Treason
FDR and the Communist Takeover of the United States

J. Goldberg

ISBN 978-0-9906463-6-5

Printed in the United States of America

Treason

FDR and the Communist Takeover of the United States

TABLE OF CONTENTS

Introduction

No, the title of this book is not a misprint. The original title for the book was to be the Greatest Mistake in the History of the World, but as I did more research, it became evident that the actions taken by President Roosevelt and his administration were not mistakes but deliberate acts. Initially, the greatest mistake appeared to be the appeasement and capitulation of the United States, which allowed Stalin to dictate the actions of the United States before, during and after World War II, and allowing the Soviet Union to develop atomic weapons. After reviewing the facts, one can only conclude that the people in the government at the time were either the most ignorant, uninformed people to ever hold public office, or they were complicit with the international socialists, and their goal of a one world socialist order.

To understand what led to the communist takeover of the United States, it is helpful to understand the political-economic foundations of socialism. In the first section, The Origins Of Evil, the political-economic system of socialism and the ideology of communism will be reviewed. The faith-based belief in Marxist doctrine, which is the basis of communism, has contributed more to human misery than any other belief system ever created.

Once the theory of Marxism is understood, one next has to look at how these ideas were implemented in the real world. There were various attempts at implementing socialism before Lenin and the Bolsheviks came to power in Russia, none of which were successful. The victory of the Bolsheviks was the beginning of what was to become a quest for world socialism. After Lenin's death this quest was furthered by Stalin.

It is hard to believe that anyone at the time was ignorant of who Lenin and Stalin were. In the second section, Lenin and Stalin: The World Knew, the truth about these two historical figures is reviewed. This section also makes the case that the world did in fact know the true nature of these men, and either chose to ignore it for either personal or political gain, or they were true believers themselves, and saw these two men as a means to achieve the ultimate goal of world socialism.

In the third section, The Soviet Union and World War II, the actions of the United States and its primary focus on Soviet assistance are reviewed. It is hard to imagine that tactical and strategic decisions made during the war were merely mistakes or poor judgment. The duration of the war and the number of lives lost were a direct result of the decisions made by the Roosevelt administration.

The fourth section, China and Korea, reviews the mistakes related to China's role in World War II and the resulting victory of the Chinese Communists over the Nationalists as a result of the failures of the Roosevelt administration. The rise of communism in China is a direct result of the support provided by the Soviet Union. The failure to stand up to the Soviets and Chinese led directly to the Korean War.

In the fifth section, The Balance of Power at the End of World War II, a brief analysis of the military and economic status of the United States and the USSR after the war is provided. At the end of World War II, the United States was clearly the only superpower both militarily and economically. It was inexcusable for the United States under the Roosevelt administration to allow Stalin to dictate the world order.

The sixth section, Betrayal and Capitulation, describes the Soviet takeover of the United States government under the Roosevelt administration. The media, left wing historians, and Roosevelt apologists have hidden the truth for decades. Just as they have hidden the truth about American history, they have concealed the truth about their Democrat (socialist) icon President Roosevelt. Now, thanks to the release of previously classified documents and several courageous authors, the truth is finally coming out.

In the final section, What Could have Been, a world that is far different than the world we live in today is described. It is a world of greater freedom, less violence and warfare, and higher living standards for all the people of the planet. Sadly, today's world leaders continue to make the same mistakes as in the past, and without a significant change in the worldview of the ruling class, things will only get worse.

The Origins of Evil

Evil is defined as anything, which produces or threatens sorrow, distress, injury, or calamity; or impairs the happiness of a being, or deprives a being of a full life; anything which causes suffering of any kind to sentient beings. A person who is evil is wicked and vicious, exhibits a complete lack of morality, and in many cases displays a total disregard for human life.

How do you measure evil? By the methods used, or the barbarity of those considered evil? By the number of people tortured or killed? Or by the number of lives ruined by the perpetrators of evil? By any measure, communism would have to qualify as the most evil ideology ever created by man. To understand this evil ideology, one has to learn about the individuals who created the ideology, and define the philosophical ideas that are the foundations of communism.

Socialism and Communism

Karl Marx (1818–1883) will be mentioned first because his ideas mark the beginning of what is erroneously referred to as scientific socialism. His ideas, presented in the works *Das Capital* and the *Communist Manifesto*, helped shape the former Soviet Union into the global leader of the socialist-communist movement. Marx believed in an idea known as the unchangeable law of history which he claimed to have discovered scientifically, although scientific method as we know it was not used in this discovery. This theory assumes that history runs in progressive stages until it reaches a final stage, that being when total communism is achieved. This final stage marks the end of history (not the end of time) in which society has reached its highest obtainable level, that being a global communistic utopia. There are six of these progressive stages, beginning with a primitive, communal state. From this state, society then progresses to a slave state, a feudal state, a capitalist state, a socialist state, and finally, to a communistic state. This simply means that each new stage of history replaces the previous stage of history until a utopian society comes into existence. Behind this process is a philosophy known as dialectical materialism, which was first conceived of by the German philosopher George Wilhelm Friedrich Hegel (1770-1831).

Dialectical materialism is the concept of progress in terms of the conflict of contradictory interacting forces called the thesis and the antithesis. It is materialist in that it denies transcendence and affirms the ultimate reality of the physical world. Since matter is the only reality, everything, including human behavior, can be explained in terms of matter, and everything has its origins in the material universe. Fundamentally, dialectical materialism means that these two opposites (the thesis and the antithesis) clash, maybe even violently, until there is a synthesis. Out of this synthesis emerges something that is better than what existed before.

As it applies to scientific socialism this process of synthesis-clash-synthesis continues until the final synthesis, that being communism begins. What this theory describes is a concept of revolutionary social change. For Marx, the thesis and the antithesis were the Bourgeois and the Proletariat respectively; the Bourgeois being the owners of the means of production, and the Proletariat being the workers who do not own the means of production. From the *Communist Manifesto*, Marx states, "The other Proletarian parties, formation of the Proletariat into a class, overthrow of the Bourgeois supremacy, and conquest of political power by the Proletariat."

Following this idea of the dialectic, where opposites clash resulting in a synthesis, today the two major forces in conflict are capitalism and communism. The Soviet communists saw communism and capitalism locked in a deadly conflict that they planned to win at all costs. To achieve their goal of winning the communist-capitalist conflict they were prepared to use any and all means available to them. As another Soviet hero, Vladimir Lenin (1870-1924) once said, "We must use any ruse, dodge, trick, cunning, unlawful methods, deceit, and veiling of the truth...for as long as capitalism and socialism exist, we cannot live in peace."

Since Lenin's ideas contribute so much to the overall ideology of the Soviets, it is worthwhile to look at a few more of his ideas. One of the major contributions of Lenin was to give the Soviets the self-proclaimed role as the world's premier communist power and leader. Another statement from Lenin that sums up the Soviet intentions and shows them in their true light is as follows: "The victorious Proletariat in one country...after organizing its own Socialist production, should stand up against the remaining capitalist world, attracting to itself the oppressed classes of other countries, raising revolts in those countries against the capitalists, and in the event of necessity, coming out even with armed force against the exploiting classes and their governments." This was a declaration of war against all governments that were not socialistic and did not adhere to the ideals prescribed by Marxist-Leninist theory.

Because socialism and communism are often used interchangeably and there is some confusion as to what precisely these terms represent, the definition of these terms and the elements that make a system either socialistic or communistic will be given.

Communism is defined as the final stage in Marxist theory in which all economic goods are distributed equally, thereby resulting in the communal ownership of property. The state withers away, which means that eventually, political organizations and operations dry up and disappear and a dictatorship of the Proletariat takes its place. Communism is not an economic theory as such, but more closely related to a political theory in the sense that it is a utopian philosophy that could never exist. There are many reasons behind the improbability of such a system being implemented. A few of the many faults of communism are given below.

First of all, the ideas of the state withering away and the dictatorship of the Proletariat taking over are ridiculous. If the massive state bureaucracy that now exists in Socialist countries were eliminated, there would be no one left to implement the various plans and programs designed for the people. In fact, the state organizations and institutions that make up the bureaucracies of the Socialist countries have been getting consistently larger. What this farfetched scheme really amounts to is that instead of a massive bureaucracy running things, a small elite class will run everything; so much for

Marx's classless society. Second, the idea that you can implement a system in which all goods and services are distributed equally among the populace is inconceivable. There is no known system that could even come close to carrying out this objective. There will always be someone, somewhere, that managed to get more. Even if you could change human nature, the logistical problems involved would be exceedingly difficult. The growth of the black market in the former Soviet Union and other socialist countries is a prime example of how unrealistic this goal is.

Socialism is more of an economic system than a political system, and like communism, it is a stage in Marx's theory of social development. The economic system of socialism seeks to accomplish three major goals. The first of these goals is the abolishment of capitalistic economic structures including the dispossession of private owners of economic institutions and facilities. This means that the government would take over and manage these institutions and facilities instead of the private sector. The second goal is the nationalization and collectivization of agriculture. The third goal is the inauguration of centralized national economic planning. The flaws inherent in socialism are far too numerous to be covered in this book, which is not meant to be a book on comparative economics. The important fact here is that only when the rest of the world becomes socialist will the true state of communism be possible.

Socialist systems inevitably lead to totalitarian systems. Totalitarianism is a political regime based on subordination of the individual to the state; characterized by strict and total control over all phases of society, such as communications and the economy; accompanied by an official ideology and a system of terrorist police control.

It is hard to imagine that people still believe in anarchism, socialism and communism. It is even harder to believe that when in 1999 the BBC conducted a poll asking people to name the greatest men and women of the millennium, the people's choice for "greatest thinker" was Karl Marx. How can anyone with any intelligence call a person who was a fanatic and who was wrong on almost every idea a great thinker?

Apparently, confusion is pervasive in Britain. Although they point out many of the flaws of Marx's theories, *The Economist* news magazine, the left-wing publication and international mouthpiece of the US Democrat Party, believes that Marx was a "brilliant thinker" and a" brilliant writer". [1]

Greatest thinker and brilliant are not typically terms you would apply to someone who was totally incorrect on all their major theories and predictions. However, ignorance, uninformed blind faith, and unsubstantiated wishful thinking are common in today's world. Many of these people believe that somehow, for some unknown reason, reality will dramatically change, and they will be proven correct. The truth is, Marx was far from brilliant, as *The Truth About Karl Marx,* by political scientist J. R. Miller points out below:

Even Karl Marx's friend Friedrich Engels, concluded that Marx was a radical revolutionary whose great aim in life was the overthrow of capitalist society and the state institutions, which it had created. Marx was the son of a prosperous lawyer. Engels was the son of a wealthy cotton manufacturer. Marx fathered six children, only three survived to grow up and of the three, two committed suicide. Having zero moral fiber, Marx fathered an illegitimate son with Helen Demuth, the longtime family maid. Fearing that this indiscretion would destroy his marriage and damage his public image, Marx and Engels organized an effective cover-up.

Marx was unable to hold a job, and with a family to support he lived a life of poverty, privation, and misfortune, which contributed heavily to his hatred and bitterness towards the capitalist system. Only handouts from the wealthy Engels saved the Marx family from starvation. Marx's claim to fame is the 1848 pamphlet *The Communist Manifesto,* which is nothing more than revolutionary propaganda calling for the violent overthrow of the whole contemporary social order.

From this miserable existence, Marx became delusional and filled with hate, as he spent 18 years working on the mostly incoherent *Das Capital.* Marx believed that his work was scientific, although it had no basis in science. Marx falsely claimed that *Das Capital* followed scientific method, which contributed immensely to his wide acceptance. He used such tricks as tying his class struggle theory of history to Darwin's theory of evolution in a feeble attempt to give his ideas respectability.

Marx's theory was based on dialectical materialism, which maintains that everything in the world is in a constant state of change. Progress is achieved by the reaction of opposing forces on each other. This led Marx to his invalid theory of historical materialism. Marx believed that the history of mankind is primarily the story of the exploitation of one class by another. Applying his ridiculous idea of dialectical materialism, he believed that the dictatorship of the proletariat followed by communal ownership and return to a classless society was inevitable.

In addition to dialectical materialism, Marx came up with additional ridiculous theories such as the theory of labor value, the theory of surplus value, and the inevitable destruction of the middle class. The theory of labor value asserted that labor is the source of all value. Value is derived from demand and utility, not from labor. As has been suggested "Men dive for pearls because they are valuable, pearls are not valuable because men dive for them." The theory of surplus value assumes that the actual value of labor was invariably in excess of wages paid. This nonsensical argument follows the idea that a workingman paid a wage of forty dollars a day actually earned that sum in six hours, but was required to work ten hours. The extra four hours, therefore, were stolen from the worker by the capitalist, proving that the capitalist system is nothing more than an evil scheme set up to exploit and to rob the working class. Although factually invalid, this concept does have value for the purposes of propaganda and agitation. Finally, the destruction of the middle class has not occurred, and the size of the middle class in most developed capitalist societies continues to increase. Capitalism is actually the creator of the middle class, not its destroyer.

Ultimately Marx was a failure in life and a failure at economics. His works have become the bible of radicals who follow it as a faith-based religion devoid of facts and evidence. Marx's neurotic ramblings on the plight of the workingman and the rise of the machines as a tool to further enslave the working class have found a small niche of believers who blindly accept the dogma of their religion and the prophet Marx. These mindless believers still dream of a Marxian utopia that will never appear.

With his insane envy of anyone with more than him, and his jealousy of power, Marx has caused more death, misery, degradation and despair than any other prophet who has ever lived. Marxian prophecy is dead; it is time for his followers to awaken to the bliss of reality.

Most of Marx's work was written in a fog of unreality and much of his published works including *The Communist Manifesto* and *Das Capital* were ghost written by Frederick Engels. Marx claimed that his system was predictive. It was, after all, in his feeble mind science. But all of his main predictions were hopeless failures. These include the demise of capitalism; that the Bolshevik Revolution in Russia would be the starting point for a proletarian revolution and communist development in the West; that class warfare would lead to revolution, class warfare is now only a political tool of the left; that the growing polarization of classes would lead to the disappearance of the middle class, when in fact there has been an increase in the middle class in almost all industrialized democracies; that the proletarian revolution was inevitable, even though it has never occurred; that there would be an inevitable decline of profits and the hampering of technical progress under capitalism, obviously just the opposite has occurred. Then there is the idea that the right to private property exists only because it serves the bourgeois, which is again another fallacy. In reality, the lack of property rights is a primary generator of poverty. One only has to look at countries where there is no right to private property to see the failure of this idea.

Beyond the fact that communism is a utopian ideal that could never exist in reality, Marx never actually took the trouble to describe how the communism he predicted and advocated would actually work. Today's anti-capitalists and global socialists proceed in much the same way. They have no concrete or even theoretical alternative to the capitalist economic system. They are simply dissatisfied with a system they don't understand and because of personal, family, or social frustrations, and political idealism, they long for what in their minds is a more just form of social organization. Instead, they invoke a utopian world free of environmental stress, social injustice, and low paying jobs, harking back to a pre-industrial golden age that never actually existed. The anti-capitalists and the global socialists have inherited more from Marx, including the self-righteous anger, the violent rhetoric, the resort to actual violence, the support of anarchism and revolution, a disdain for democracy and free markets, the demonization of big business, and the division of the world into exploiters and victims. Marx was not a scientist, he founded a faith, and his secular religion lives on.

Dr. Fred Schwarz, in his classic book *You can Trust the Communists to be Communists*, provides perhaps the best description of the communists; "The communists are not hypocrites. They suffer from paranoiac delusions of intense sincerity. They are so enmeshed in the delusions of Marxism-Leninism that they are beyond the scope of rational argument and conviction. All observed phenomena are interpreted within the framework of their preconceived conclusions. If they were hypocrites, it would be much easier to deal with them."

Dr. Schwarz continues, "Hitler worked on the principle: tell a lie, make it big, repeat it often, and the majority of the people will believe you. The communists have further developed this concept. Any lie that advances communist conquest is, by definition not a lie but the Marxist-Leninist truth." [2]

When dealing with the communists (socialists) and you want to know the truth, whenever a communist makes a statement, take the opposite and you will have the truth. For example, the left always states that Roosevelt saved capitalism from communism with the New Deal when the opposite is true, he saved communism and destroyed capitalism. If you want to separate the truth from fake news consider the source. If the source is the left, take the opposite of whatever they say and you will have the truth.

Lenin and Stalin: The World Knew

The philosophy of communism was developed by Marx and Engels. There were other contributors to socialist thought before Marx and Engels but it was Marxism that formed the basis of revolutionary thought for Lenin. It was Lenin who would be the first to implement the ideals of Marxism in what became the Bolshevik revolution. The end product of the revolution and Lenin's implementation of Marxism resulted in what is now referred to as Marxist-Leninist doctrine. To understand the Soviet Union, you have to understand the origin of Soviet Russia and the role Lenin had in forming the totalitarian state.

The Truth about Lenin

Vladimir Ulyanov, known as Lenin, was born on April 10, 1870, to an upper middle-class family in the small provincial town of Simbirsk, Russia. Lenin had a normal childhood and enjoyed reading and chess, and didn't show any early inclination towards politics. The death of his father at an early age was a terrible blow to his family, but it would be another tragedy that would lead him down the path of the revolutionary.

Lenin was filled with rage after his older brother Alexander Ulyanov, who was involved in a plot to assassinate Tsar Alexander III, was hanged at the age of twenty-one. From that moment on, Lenin's primary objective was for a socialist revolution in Russia, and the removal of the Tsarist regime.

After a brief period as a lawyer, Lenin became a full time revolutionary. He studied Marx and other radical writers and began to write papers and books on revolutionary tactics and organization. His best-known work, *What is to be Done*? had a big impact on the Marxist radical movement and propelled him to a leadership role in the revolutionary socialist movement in Russia. *What is to be Done*? was the bible of Lenin's Bolsheviks, the blueprint for how he would seize and hold power. It was a manual for imposing dictatorship, but not in true Marxist form as the dictatorship of the proletariat, it was the dictatorship over the proletariat.

Like Adolf Hitler, in his *Mein Kamp*, where he formulated Nazism, Lenin, in 1902, published *What is to be Done*? in which he formulated the basic doctrine of what would become Bolshevism. Lenin rejected Marx's theory that given time the working class was bound to revolt. Lenin believed that left to itself, the working class was unwilling and incapable of moving beyond trade unionism. Professional revolutionaries full of revolutionary zeal from outside the working class had to be brought in for a revolution to occur. Lenin desired a party organized on military lines, composed of professional revolutionaries' subject to maximum discipline and indoctrination. He desired a party of total obedience and submission that would operate with a single mind and will.[3]

Lenin was always domineering, abusive, combative and often downright vicious. He battered opponents into submission with the deliberate use of violent language which he acknowledged was 'calculated to evoke hatred, aversion, contempt ... not to convince, not to correct the mistakes of the opponent but to destroy him, to wipe him and his organization off the face of the earth'.[4] Abusive language, harsh criticism, and character assassination, remain the preferred tools of the political left today.

Lenin knew that the Bolshevik Party had limited support, and brutal methods would be required to maintain power. Lenin would ask, 'how can you make a revolution without firing squads?' To implement his Red terror, he needed a terror organization. His solution was the formation of the Cheka, the foundation of the Soviet police state, later to become the feared KGB. The Cheka would dispense 'revolutionary justice'. Even though Lenin referred to the Cheka as 'the Party's sword and shield', the Cheka answered only to Lenin, not the Party.

Lenin was willing to do whatever was necessary to further the socialist revolution, including becoming a traitor to his country. He sold out to the Germans. He wanted Russia to lose the war because he thought defeat would be a spark for revolution. He made a secret deal with the Germany, which funneled large amounts of money to the Bolsheviks, and allowed him to return to Russia from exile in Switzerland in the so called 'sealed train' journey. Even Lenin's fellow leftists were outraged that he would make a deal with the German militarists and imperialists.

Lenin, like his prophet Marx, lived like a true communist, a parasite living off the backs of others. He mainly lived off donations from wealthy Russians, and was constantly begging for more funds from his mother.

The Bolsheviks could not rely solely on donations from millionaire magnates to finance the revolution. Lenin formed a criminal gang to steal on the Party's behalf, what he called expropriations. Lenin appointed Leonid Krasin, and his right-hand man Joseph Stalin as gang leaders. The various gangs they employed stole a large sum of cash and gold from the safe aboard the steamship Nicholas I, and attacked post offices and state railway ticket offices.

Making revolution was an expensive business and Lenin always needed money. He even came up with an elaborate plan to swindle two teenage girls out of their inheritance. He would order his fellow thug Stalin to rob banks whenever he needed money to finance his criminal empire, at one point using his armed goons to rob the National Bank of five million rubles to start the Soviet Treasury.

Lenin was not interested in extravagant living, but for the revolution he was prepared to lie, steal, cheat and kill for money to further Bolshevik interests. 'Everything that is done in the interests of the proletarian cause is honest,' he told the Italian communist and Secretary of the Communist International (Comintern), Angelica Balabanova.[5]

Lenin's dream of a worldwide socialist revolution began with the Bolshevik revolution of October 1917. The Bolsheviks won because the other side was even more incompetent and divided than they were, and things were so bad in Russia at the time that most people didn't care which side won. In fact, few people realized anything significant had happened until it was all over.[6]

After the revolution, no individual or group was immune from Lenin's wrath. Lenin needed enemies to rally his comrades. One way of accomplishing this was through class warfare. He invented a new class of

Russians, the kulaks or rich peasants, whom he claimed were hoarding grain and deliberately starving the rest of the country. The fact that there were no 'rich' peasants did not matter. Lenin's solution to the kulak problem; requisition brigades, who would surround villages and demand that peasants' hand over a set yield of grain decided by the local Bolshevik Party headquarters. The result, at least 3,700 people killed in the first year of the grain requisitions.

During the famine there were peasant revolts throughout the country. During the Kronstadt uprising Lenin authorized the use of poison gas. The Red Army burned villages and took no prisoners, and the rebellion was quickly crushed.

Lenin lived comfortably during the earlier Volga region famine of 1891, in which more than 400,000 people, almost all of them peasants, starved to death. Even though Lenin lived in the famine-stricken areas, he would have nothing to do with relief or charitable work to help the dying peasants. For him, the important thing was that the famine would weaken the autocracy and might further the cause of the revolution.[7]

Lenin was a fanatical revolutionary determined to destroy the existing social and political order. The source of Lenin's revolutionary passion was not sympathy for the poor; indeed, when famine struck the Volga region in 1891-92, he alone among the local intelligentsia opposed humanitarian assistance to the starving peasants, on the grounds that the famine was progressive because it destroyed the old peasant economy and paved the way for socialism.[8]

The kulaks were not the only ones to suffer during the famine. Lenin created another enemy, the church. He had wanted to destroy religion in Russia and the famine provided the opportunity. He blamed the churches for hoarding treasure that could have been used to purchase grain. Lenin sent Cheka officers to loot the churches.

This was the violent beginning of the suppression of religion in Russia, which over the next fifteen years saw more than 97 percent of the Soviet Union's churches, synagogues, and mosques closed down. Within two years of Lenin's edict, more than thirty bishops and 1,200 priests had been killed and thousands more jailed.

The following is from *The Unknown Lenin: From the Secret Archive* (1996), Edited by Richard Pipes, the entry is dated March 1922:

"It is precisely now and only now, when in the starving regions people are eating human flesh and hundreds if not thousands of corpses are littering the roads, that we can (and therefore must) ..." At this point the unversed reader might pause to wonder how the sentence will go forward. Something like "pursue all avenues of amelioration and relief," perhaps?

But no. This is Vladimir Ilyich Lenin, the leader of "a party of a new type," who continues: "... carry out the confiscation of church valuables with the most savage and merciless energy. ... Precisely at this moment we must give battle to [the clergy] in the most decisive and merciless manner and crush its resistance with such brutality that it will not forget it for decades to come. ... The greater the number of representatives of the reactionary clergy and reactionary bourgeoisie we succeed in executing for this reason, the better." Church records show that 1,962 monks, 2,691 priests and 3,447 nuns were killed in that year alone. Religion, you see, was part of human nature, so the Bolsheviks were obliged to suppress it in all its forms.

Lenin finally got his revenge for the death of his brother when he signed the execution order for Tsar Nicholas II and his family. The entire family, including the Russian Imperial Romanov family (Tsar Nicholas II, his wife Tsarina Alexandra and their five children Olga, Tatiana, Maria, Anastasia, and Alexei) were shot, bayoneted and clubbed to death. Their bodies were looted then stripped, mutilated, burned and disposed of in a field called Porosenkov Log in the Koptyaki forest. The following night The Grand Duchess Ella, who had become a nun, her companion Sister Barbara, Grand Duke Sergei and five other Romanovs were murdered, again at the hands of Lenin's secret police, the Cheka.[9]

Lenin was dictating orders right up to his death on January 21, 1924, at the age of 54. Like many arrogant and dominant leaders, Lenin and his followers believed that he was irreplaceable, and there were no official plans for his successor. Except for his wife Nadya (Nadezhda Krupskaya), and his mistress Inessa Armand, Lenin had no true friends, only people who were useful to him.

The two top Bolsheviks after Lenin were Trotsky and Stalin. Lenin had promoted Stalin to the top position in the Party, creating the post of General Secretary specifically for him. This position gave Stalin a large power base within the Party and he took full advantage of it.

Stalin learned well from his communist master Lenin. Using the same ruthless tactics of his mentor, Stalin became the new Soviet dictator until his death in 1953. Trotsky was expelled from the party, exiled, and eventually assassinated on orders from Stalin. To understand the history of Russia from the time of Lenin's death to the start of World War II and its immediate aftermath, it is helpful to understand the man who led the Soviet Union during that period.

The Truth about Stalin

Joseph (Iosif) Vissarionovich Stalin was a Soviet revolutionary and dictator. Governing the Soviet Union from the mid-1920s until his death in 1953, he served as General Secretary of the Central Committee of the Communist Party of the Soviet Union from 1922 to 1952, and as Premier of the Soviet Union from 1941 to 1953.

Stalin was born on December 21, 1897, in Gori, Georgia. His father was a shoemaker and died when Stalin was 11 years old. He was raised by his mother who wanted him to become a priest in the Georgian Orthodox Church. He actually attended the seminary, until he became a Marxist. After his brief encounter with Christianity, Stalin became a revolutionary propagandist and agitator. As a result of his revolutionary activities he was arrested several times by the Tsarist regime.

Like Marx and Lenin, Stalin was a man with zero moral fiber. Stalin was married and had affairs with many other women, and had at least two illegitimate children, although he never recognized them as being his.

Stalin was never an orator or polemicist like Trotsky or Lenin, Stalin specialized in the basics of revolutionary activity; organizing workers, distributing illegal literature, and robbing banks and trains to support the socialist cause. He was looked upon as a man of action and an organizer, not a theoretician. Elevation to higher positions in the Bolshevik party was in many cases predicated upon the ability to prove that you were more ruthless than other party members. Stalin excelled at being ruthless. If Stalin decided you were a counter-revolutionary, he would simply have you executed, no proof or trial required.

For Stalin, the civil war was especially formative, since it gave him his first experience of executive power. In 1918, he was sent to the city of Tsaritsyn, strategically situated along the Volga River and the site of an important rail junction. His mission was to secure food for the starving workers of Moscow and Petrograd—to confiscate grain, in other words, and to serve, in effect, as the "Bolshevik bandit-in-chief." To meet the challenge, he granted himself military powers, took over the local branch of the secret police, and stole 10 million rubles from another group of Bolsheviks. When the rail lines failed to function as he wished, he executed the local technical specialists, calling them "class aliens."

His disposition of other suspected counter-revolutionaries, "did not flow from sadism or panic, but was a political strategy, to galvanize the workers and intimidate would be anti-Bolsheviks," warning his followers that internal foes of the revolution were about to stage a rebellion, recapture the city, and hand it over to the White Army: "Here, in tiniest embryo, was the scenario of countless fabricated trials of the 1920s and 30s." [10]

Marxist-Leninist ideology offered Stalin a deep sense of certainty in the face of political and economic setbacks. If policies designed to produce prosperity created poverty instead, an explanation could always be found: the theory had been incorrectly interpreted, the forces were not correctly aligned, or the officials had blundered. If Soviet policies were unpopular, even among workers, that too could be explained: antagonism was rising because the class struggle was intensifying. The communists never admit that socialism or communism doesn't work. It is always some vast capitalist or imperialist conspiracy that is at fault, or whatever they were trying to accomplish that wasn't working, was due to the fact they were just not doing enough of it.

Whatever went wrong, the counter-revolution, the forces of conservatism, the secret influence of the bourgeoisie could always be held responsible. These beliefs were further reinforced by the searing battles of 1918–20 between the Red and White Armies. Over and over again, Stalin learned that violence was the key to success. "Civil war was not something that deformed the Bolsheviks; it formed them, indeed it saved them from near oblivion of 1918. The Civil war provided the opportunity to develop and to validate the struggle against 'exploiting classes' and 'enemies' (domestic and international), thereby imparting a sense of seeming legitimacy, urgency, and moral fervor to predatory methods. "The ruling class," as Lenin explained, "never turns its power over to the downtrodden class."[11]

Lenin brought Stalin into the Bolshevik central committee, and Stalin became the first editor of *Pravda*, the Bolshevik newspaper. Lenin promoted Stalin to the top position in the Party, creating the post of General Secretary specifically for him. This position gave Stalin a large power base within the Party and he took full advantage of it. After Lenin's death, Stalin consolidated power and seized total control. Stalin learned well from his communist master Lenin. Using the same ruthless tactics of his mentor, Stalin became the new Soviet dictator until his death.

Stalin orchestrated the arrest and show trials of many former opponents in the Communist Party: denounced as Western-backed mercenaries, many were imprisoned or sent to one of the many forced labor camps in the Gulag system. The first Moscow Trial took place in August 1936. Lev Kamenev and Grigory Zinoviev were among those accused of plotting assassinations, found guilty in a show trial, and executed. The second Moscow Trial took place in January 1937, and the third in March 1938, in which Nikolai Bukharin and Alexei Rykov were accused of involvement in the alleged Trotskyite-Zinovievite terrorist plot and sentenced to death. It did not matter that all these men were former allies and Bolshevik revolutionaries, Stalin executed former allies and rivals alike. For Stalin, power was all that mattered.

By late 1937, all remnants of collective leadership were gone from the Politburo, which was controlled entirely by Stalin. There were mass expulsions from the party, with Stalin commanding foreign communist parties to also purge anti-Stalinist elements. During the 1930s and 1940s, the NKVD (The People's Commissariat for Internal Affairs) assassinated defectors and opponents abroad. In August 1940, Trotsky was assassinated in Mexico, eliminating the last of Stalin's opponents among the former Party leadership. These purges were followed by the arrest of members of the military Supreme Command and additional mass arrests throughout the military, often on fabricated charges. These purges replaced most of the party's old guard with younger officials who did not remember a time before Stalin's leadership and who were regarded as more personally loyal to him.

Stalin's tyranny intensified in December 1936, and remained at a high level until November 1938, a period known as the Great Purge. By the latter part of 1937, the purges had moved beyond the party and were affecting the wider population. In July 1937, the Politburo ordered a purge of "anti-Soviet elements" in society, affecting Bolsheviks who had opposed Stalin, former Mensheviks and Socialist Revolutionaries, priests, former soldiers in the White Army, and common criminals. Stalin and

Yezhov signed Order No. 00447, listing 268,950 people for arrest, of whom 75,950 were executed. He also initiated "national operations", the ethnic cleansing of non-Soviet ethnic groups—among them Poles, Germans, Latvians, Finns, Greeks, Koreans, and Chinese - through internal or external exile. During these years, approximately 1.6 million people were arrested, 700,000 were shot, and an unknown number died under NKVD torture.[12] Along with Hitler and Mao, Stalin was one of the evilest men in the history of civilization, one who ordered the systematic killing of people on a massive scale.

After a long series of purges and expulsions Stalin succeeded in transforming the Communist International (Comintern) into a monolithic organization identifying the interests of world communism with Stalin's dogma and policies. Stalin's ultimate goal was world domination and world socialism. Always the professional revolutionary, Generalissimo Stalin, would keep fighting until the final defeat of international capitalism was achieved. With the assistance of the Roosevelt administration he almost succeeded.

Stalin died from a cerebral hemorrhage at the Kremlin on March 5, 1953, at the age 73. Like Lenin, Stalin left no anointed successor or a framework within which a transfer of power could take place. The Central Committee met on the day of his death, with Malenkov, Beria, and Khrushchev emerging as the party's key figures. It was Khrushchev who then led the Soviet Union and directed the Cold War as the First Secretary of the Communist Party of the Soviet Union from 1953 to 1964.[13,14,15]

The truth about these two Soviet dictators was well known. The evil, brutal, tyranny of their totalitarian state was well known. Only another communist would ignore the evil of these men and their totalitarian regimes. Only another communist would come to their aid and save them from certain destruction.

Russian Communism

Marxist-Leninist theory became reality as a result of the Bolshevik Revolution of October 1917, in Russia. Communism did not come to Russia as a result of a popular uprising, only 5.3 percent of industrial workers belonged to the Bolshevik Party. Rather a dictatorship was imposed on the country by a small minority hiding behind democratic slogans. Without a popular mandate the dictatorship soon became a brutal totalitarian regime.

Like the communists and politicians of today, Lenin promised the people everything and delivered nothing; nothing that is except misery for the majority of the populace. For the socialist revolution the end always justifies the means.

Lenin and his clones always speak of social and economic inequality. Their solution to inequality is confiscation of private property, nationalization of commercial enterprises, stealing the land and requisitioning the grain of peasants, looting churches, synagogues and mosques, and executing anyone who does not agree with them. Once these programs have been completed and they have created an elite ruling class then, as George Orwell said in *Animal Farm*, "everyone is equal, but some are more equal than others."

Within a few months of the revolution, the Russian writer Gorky was writing to his wife that only the commissars (Party members) lead a pleasant life these days. They steal as much as they can from the ordinary people in order to pay for their courtesans and their un-socialist luxuries.

Since the time of the pharaohs, state officials looked after themselves and formed an interest group in many instances more influential than the propertied class. After the communist takeover by Lenin, the Supreme Council of the National Economy, the organization in charge of industry, in 1921 employed 250,000 officials and this at a time when industrial productivity had dropped to below one fifth of its 1913 level. By 1928, the party and state bureaucracy came to number 4 million.[16]

Just like today, the communists joined the bureaucracy because a government job assured them a modicum of security and livelihood, and like today, government workers have greater benefits than the private sector, they have free health care, generous pensions, and typically can never be fired, so they have a job for life. Before long, the ruling class came to constitute a caste that placed its collective interests above not only those of the population at large, but those of the communist cause that they nominally served.

The failures of communism are many. One of the most tragic failures is in agriculture. The communist policies of confiscation of private property and collectivization caused famines of unprecedented scale. Communist induced famines occurred in the Soviet Union, China, Cambodia, Ethiopia, and North Korea; in each of these countries millions of people died from man-made starvation.

The nationalization of all productive assets turns all citizens into state employees' dependent on the government. In the words of Trotsky: "In a country where the sole employer is the state, opposition means slow starvation. The old principle, who does not work shall not eat, has been replaced by a new one: who does not obey shall not eat." [17]

After reading the truth about Lenin and Stalin you may not be convinced that Lenin and Stalin were evil men. Perhaps you would agree that using famine as a weapon would be considered evil. The Soviet famine of 1932–33 was a major famine that killed millions of people in the major grain-producing areas of the Soviet Union, including Ukraine, Northern Caucasus, Volga Region and Kazakhstan, the South Urals, and West Siberia.[18,19] The Holodomor in Ukraine and Kazakh famine of 1932–33 have been seen as genocide committed by Stalin and his comrades. It is estimated between 3.3 and 7.5 million died in Ukraine and ~2,000,000 (40% of all Kazakhs) died in Kazakhstan.[20,21,22,23]

Using famine as weapon was not constrained to Russia. The estimated 4 million deaths that resulted from hunger in 1932 and 1933 were part of a deliberate campaign by Stalin and the Bolshevik leadership to crush Ukrainian national aspirations, literally starving actual or potential bearers of those aspirations into submission to the Soviet order.

The Bolsheviks, were driven by "a combination of ideas or habits of thought, especially profound antipathy to markets and all things bourgeois, as well as no-holds-barred revolutionary methods."[24] Right after the revolution, these convictions led them to outlaw private trade, nationalize industry, confiscate property, seize grain and redistribute it in the cities—all policies that required mass violence to implement. In 1918, Lenin himself suggested that peasants should be forced to deliver their grain to the state, and that those who refused should be "shot on the spot."

Communist regimes thrive on crises. Crises alone permitted the authorities to demand and obtain total submission, and all necessary sacrifices from its citizens. The system needed sacrifices and sacrificial victims for the good of the cause and the happiness of future generations. Crises enabled the system in this way to build a bridge from the fictional world of utopian programs to the world of reality.[25]

With a collapsing economy and famine, Lenin concluded that brutal force was not enough to achieve his socialist utopia. In 1921, he announced the introduction of the New Economic Policy (NEP). Leninist theoretical justification of the NEP argued that the Soviet Union had not gone deeply enough into the capitalist phase and therefore needed limited capitalism in order to fully evolve its means of production. The key provision was the abandonment of forcible extractions of food; the peasants were henceforth to pay a tax in kind and allowed to sell their surplus on the open market. The government also authorized a limited amount of trade and private manufacture of consumer goods. Strict state control remained in place.[26]

Like the Russian communists, in order for the Chinese communists to maintain power they had to introduce a new economic policy of their own. The former leader of the People's Republic of China, Deng Xiaoping, argued that China was in the primary stage of socialism and that the duty of the party was to perfect so-called "socialism with Chinese characteristics."

The goals of Deng's reforms were summed up by the Four Modernizations, those of agriculture, industry, science and technology, and the military. The strategy for achieving these aims of becoming a modern, industrial nation was the socialist market economy. China has tried to combine the strength of the market's invisible hand with the visible hand of state intervention to correct what they believe are market failures.

Despite all their babbling about destroying capitalism, all communists eventually learn the lesson that at least limited capitalism must be allowed if they want to maintain power, create a modern state, and produce wealth and economic growth. Lenin and Deng Xiaoping are just two examples.

Once the socialist revolution in Russia was complete, Lenin always believed that world revolution was just around the corner that 'the interests of socialism, of world socialism, are superior to national interests, the interests of the state.' To reach the long-term goal of world socialism, Lenin created the Third International or the Communist International (Comintern). The Comintern was an international communist organization that advocated world communism.

The Bolsheviks seized power in Russia only because it was a target of opportunity. They had no intention of staying within its borders, convinced that their revolution would be crushed by the combined forces of world capitalism unless it rapidly spread to the industrial countries of the West. Lenin put it bluntly: "We have always emphasized that one cannot achieve such a task as a socialist revolution in one country." In a speech delivered in 1920, he made the foreign dimension of the Russian Revolution unmistakably clear:

[In November 1917] we knew that our victory will be a lasting victory only when our undertaking will conquer the whole world, because we had launched it exclusively counting on the world revolution.[27]

The Comintern resolved at its Second Congress to "struggle by all available means, including armed force, for the overthrow of the international bourgeoisie and the creation of an international Soviet republic as a transition stage to the complete abolition of the state."[28]

American Communism

Socialism in the United States began with utopian communities in the early 19th century such as the Shakers, Robert Owen's socialist experiment at New Harmony, and intentional communities inspired by Charles Fourier. The term socialism was coined by the followers of Robert Owen in the late 1820's.

Owen was a British industrialist and founder of New Harmony. Owen's socialist philosophy was derived from two fundamental pillars of his thought. The first was that no human "is responsible for his will and his own actions."

The second pillar, a natural complement to the first, was a fierce opposition to religion. "There is no sacrifice ... which I ... would not have ... willing and joyously made to terminate the existence of religion on earth," he declared.

New Harmony ran into problems since its inception. Few skilled workmen were attracted to New Harmony. Owen and others complained that the streets were filled with idlers and there was irregularity of effort, which led to bickering. One member of the community remarked that "instead of striving who should do most, the most industry was manifested in accusing others of doing little." Due to the lack of willing workers, the committee gave up all idea of farming, except the sowing of fifty or sixty acres for winter barley, which they wisely concluded would be wanted for their beer the ensuing year. The only things that seemed to be pursued with energy at New Harmony were meetings and entertainment.

Owens son, Robert Dale Owen, concluded on the collapse of New Harmony "the most potent factor" was that "All cooperative schemes which provide equal remuneration to the skilled and industrious and the ignorant and idle, must work their own downfall, for by this unjust plan of remuneration they must of necessity eliminate the valuable members – who find their service reaped by the indigent – and retain only the improvident, unskilled, and vicious members."[29]

Charles Fourier (1772–1837) was a French philosopher, influential early socialist thinker, and one of the founders of utopian socialism. Some of Fourier's social and moral views, held to be radical in his lifetime, have become mainstream thinking in modern society. Fourier is, for instance, credited with having originated the word feminism in 1837. Fourier's disciples organized settlements in the United States such as The North American Phalanx, which was a secular utopian socialist commune.

Socialism found new adherents when labor activists - usually British, German, or Jewish immigrants - founded the Socialist Labor Party in 1877, and the Socialist Party of America was established in 1901. Communism emerged in the United States after Russian communists encouraged left wing elements to separate from the Socialist Party of America in 1919 and create a Communist Party based on Marxist-Leninist doctrine. In 1929, fractional intraparty conflict was eliminated and party discipline was restored by Moscow and the party was then recreated as an avowed section of the Communist International (Comintern). The Communist Party USA (CPUSA) has a long, complex history that is closely tied with American labor unions, civil rights organizations, and the feminist movement.

In an effort to conceal its true goal of overthrowing the government of the United States, the Communist Party revised its constitution and sought to associate itself in the public mind with American democratic traditions. They also attempted to mask the party's revolutionary ambitions and its Moscow orientation despite the fact that the Kremlin was in total control of the American Communist Party. This control is clearly demonstrated by the Moscow archives of the Comintern. As Stalin understood, the very premise of communist parties around the world was that Moscow was the New Jerusalem. To be a communist meant to accept the Kremlin's authority.[30]

The communists penetrated almost all phases of American life through a multitude of subversive fronts. Their purpose was to establish a communist government in the United States. Most of the American fronts were organized after Roosevelt's recognition of Russia in November 1933. For example:

> There were sixty-one fronts or committees engaged in political activity under such labels as "Communist Party, USA," "Communist Political Association," "United Communist Party," and "American Workers Party."

> Forty-seven were concerned with civil rights, such as "Civil Rights Federation," and "Civil Rights Congress."

> Fronts were at work at forty-seven colleges, universities, and schools, fifty-one news services, newspapers, periodicals and publications, and there are many more.[31]

In the 1960s, Michael Harrington and other socialists were called to assist the Kennedy administration and then the Johnson administration's War on Poverty and Great Society programs, while other communists used cultural Marxism and increasing government control to further the socialist revolution. As we will see, the Communist Party USA and its infiltration of the federal government reached its peak during the Roosevelt administration.

The Soviet Union and World War II

On March 31, 1939, in response to Nazi Germany's defiance of the Munich Agreement and occupation of Czechoslovakia, the United Kingdom and France pledged their support to guarantee Polish independence.

On August 25, 1939, two days after the Nazi-Soviet Pact, the Agreement of Mutual Assistance between the United Kingdom and Poland was signed. The agreement contained promises of mutual military assistance between the nations in the event either was attacked by some "European country."

The German invasion of Poland began on September 1, 1939, one week after the signing of the Molotov–Ribbentrop Pact. On September 17, 1939, the Soviet Union invaded Poland through the eastern Polish border. This was in keeping with the Molotov-Ribbentrop Pact's secret protocol specifying the division of Poland. The campaign ended on October 6, 1939, with Germany and the Soviet Union dividing and annexing the whole of Poland under the terms of the German–Soviet Frontier Treaty.

According to the Polish-British Common Defense Pact, the United Kingdom should give Poland "all the support and assistance in its power" if Poland was "engaged in hostilities with a European power in consequence of aggression by the latter." The Polish ambassador in London, Raczyñski, contacted the British Foreign Office pointing out that clause 1(b) of the agreement which concerned an "aggression by a European power" on Poland, should apply to the Soviet invasion. The Foreign Secretary Lord Halifax responded that the obligation of British Government towards Poland arising out of the Anglo-Polish Agreement, was restricted to Germany, according to the first clause of the secret protocol.[32]

Like many wars, World War II could have been a limited war. Britain and France should have never entered the war. After the German-Soviet annexation, Poland was doomed. One has to wonder, why Britain and France would sign an agreement with Poland to fight a war against Germany – a war they knew they could not win. Why would they repeat the mistakes of World War I? Beyond the fact that Britain and France should have never agreed to a common defense pact, why did the pact only apply to Nazi Germany and not Communist Russia?

The left-wing historians and Soviet sympathizers parrot the communist party line that invading sovereign nations like Finland and Poland were defensive actions to protect the Russian motherland from the western imperialists. This is nonsense and another Stalin lie. The Soviets knew the West had no plans to attack the Soviet Union. The Soviets were using military aggression to expand their territory and sphere of influence.

Evidence of Soviet imperialism comes from the Nazi-Soviet Pact of 1939, which contained secret protocols dividing Eastern Europe into German and Soviet spheres of influence. Most of Poland was to be German; the rest was to be Russian. Finland, Estonia, Lithuania, and Latvia were all to belong to Russia. The Soviet communists were just as guilty of aggression against sovereign states as the Nazis, when in 1939 – 1941 the Soviets attacked Poland, Finland, Lithuania, Latvia, Estonia, and Bessarabia. Bessarabia is a historical region in Eastern Europe, bounded by the Dniester river on the east and the Prut river on the west. Today, Bessarabia is mostly (approx. 65%) part of the modern-day Moldova, with the Ukrainian Budjak region covering the southern coastal region and part of the Ukrainian Chernivtsi Oblast covering a small area in the north.

Stalin's hatred of the Poles goes back to the Soviet-Polish War and the defeat of the Red Army at the Battle of Warsaw in 1920. Nikolai Yezhov, the head of the NKVD during the Great Terror became obsessed with imagined Polish conspiracies. Poles in the NKVD were purged, and in Order 00485 of August 1937, Poles were implicitly defined as enemies of the state. When Yezhov reported after the first twenty days of arrests, tortures and executions, Stalin praised his work: 'Very good! Keep on digging up and cleaning out this Polish filth'.[33] In the anti-Polish drives during the Great Terror, 143,810 people were arrested for espionage and 111,091 executed.[34]

While the British and French foolishly started a war with Germany, President Roosevelt was covertly making plans to engage the United States in the war. While claiming that he was not going to get America involved in the war, he was busy making secret pledges to the British and violating the Neutrality Act, which effectively made the United States a belligerent.

Roosevelt's violations of the Neutrality Act include, the Destroyers for Bases Agreement, the Lend-Lease Act, the Atlantic Charter, the occupation by American troops and transfer of military control from Britain to the United States of Iceland in July, 1941, the extension of the Pan-American Security Zone, US destroyers escorting American supply vessels bound for Britain, and orders for American warships to shoot on sight German submarines.[35]

Under the guise of keeping America out of the war, Roosevelt demanded powers in the Lend-Lease Act which, with his unique interpretation of his powers as Commander in Chief, enabled him to launch undeclared war without the approval of the American people or Congress. His representation that it was necessary to save the British Empire from Hitler and to establish freedom throughout the world was an even more stupendous violation of the truth. [36]

A review of the military situation in the world at the time Lend-Lease was passed clearly showed that Hitler had abandoned any idea of trying an invasion across the 25 miles of the English Channel in the face of the superiority of the British Navy. Hitler had been defeated five months before in his air blitz in the Battle of Britain, and the fact that Hitler's consistent ambition, intention and preparations during the previous eight years had been the conquest of Russia and Eastern Europe.[37] Nazi Germany was never a direct threat to the United States. Without American, British, and French involvement, the world stood a chance that two of the evilest dictators the world has known would destroy each other.

Roosevelt repeatedly deceived the American people. Given the non-interventionist views of the American people after World War I, any attempt to get America involved in another World War would have led to Roosevelt's defeat in the 1940 election. Roosevelt's actions were the result of blundering statesmanship, gross incompetence, adherence to socialist ideology, an attempt to cover up the failure of the New Deal, and his ambition to get reelected at any cost to satisfy his consuming desire for power. It is certain that his actions were intellectually dishonest, his statements untruthful, and his actions unconstitutional.

Lend-Lease Act

The Lend-Lease policy, formally titled An Act to Promote the Defense of the United States, (H.R. 1776, 55 Stat. 31, enacted March 11, 1941) was an American program to defeat Germany, Japan and Italy by distributing food, oil, and materiel between 1941 and August 1945. The aid went to the United Kingdom, the Soviet Union, and China. It included warships and warplanes, along with other weaponry.

The program was under the direct control of the White House, with Roosevelt and his advisor Harry Hopkins managing the allocation of resources, and ensuring that Stalin and the Russians were a top priority of the war effort. The budget was hidden away in the overall military budget, and details were not released until after the war. A total of $50.1 billion (equivalent to $681 billion presently) was involved, or 11% of the total war expenditures of the United States.[38]

In June 1941, within weeks of the German invasion of Russia, the first British aid convoy set off along the dangerous Arctic sea route to Murmansk. Arriving in September, the shipment included 40 Hawker Hurricanes along with 550 mechanics and pilots of No. 151 Wing to provide immediate air defense for the port and to train Russian pilots.

By the end of 1941, early shipments of Matilda, Valentine and Tetrarch tanks represented only 6.5% of total Soviet tank production but over 25% of medium and heavy tanks produced for the Red Army.[39,40] The

British tanks first saw action with the Russian 138th Independent Tank Battalion in the Volga Reservoir in November 1941.[41] Lend-Lease tanks constituted 30 to 40 percent of heavy and medium tank strength. Between June 1941 and May 1945, Britain delivered to Russia:

3,000+ Hurricanes
4,000+ other aircraft
27 naval vessels
5,218 tanks (including 1,380 Valentines from Canada)
5,000+ anti-tank guns
4,020 ambulances and trucks
323 machinery trucks
1,212 Universal Carriers and Loyd Carriers (with another 1,348 from Canada)
1,721 motorcycles
£1.15bn worth of aircraft engines
1,474 radar sets
4,338 radio sets
600 naval radar and sonar sets
Hundreds of naval guns
15 million pairs of boots

In all, Britain sent the Russian's 5,218 tanks that, coupled with those sent by the US, made up about 11 percent of Russia's total wartime tank production. London sent 308 million pounds sterling of armaments and another 120 million in raw materials, food and medical supplies. In dollar terms (using the then extant exchange rate), the British sent about $1.7 billion worth of supplies, 15 percent of the total aid to Russia. In total, 4 million tons of war material including food and medical supplies were delivered. In accordance with the Anglo-Soviet Military Supplies Agreement of June

1942, military aid sent from Britain to the Soviet Union during the war was entirely free of charge.[42]

Three months after the German invasion, the United States extended assistance to the Soviet Union through its Lend-Lease Act of March 1941. About $11.3 billion (equivalent to $154 billion today) in war material was sent to the Soviet Union under that program. About seventy percent of the aid reached the Soviet Union via the Persian Gulf through Iran; the remainder went across the Pacific to Vladivostok and across the North Atlantic to Murmansk. Lend-Lease to the Soviet Union officially ended in September 1945. Joseph Stalin never revealed to his own people the full contributions of Lend-Lease to their country's survival.

The US delivered 11,400 aircraft, 7,165 tanks, 5,500 40mm anti-aircraft guns, 1,000 quad-mounted 50 caliber anti-aircraft guns, 2,500 81mm mortars, 137,000 .45 caliber sub-machineguns, 4,423 P-39 Airacobras, the Americans also delivered modern aircraft such as the P-47 Thunderbolt, approximately 350,000 trucks were delivered during the course of the war. That number was equal to all of Germany's truck production during the war, and it exceeded the Soviets' own production by about 150,000 vehicles, 50 million square feet of all-weather landing mats were sent to help construct temporary airfields near the front, 1,100 locomotives, some 11,000 freight cars and 3,600 miles of track, 49,000 Jeeps and 34,000 motorcycles, nearly 300,000 pairs of rubber-soled ski boots, 400,000 Arctic suits and 1 million pairs of woolen underwear, 106 million yards of cotton cloth, 62 million yards of woolen cloth, and 14 million pairs of boots, 4.4 million tons of foodstuffs, or about 10 percent of the 40 million tons of food consumed by the Soviet armed forces during the war.[43]

The Republic P-47 Thunderbolt was a World War II era fighter aircraft produced by the United States between 1941 and 1945. Its primary armament was eight .50-caliber machine guns and in the fighter-bomber ground-attack role it could carry five-inch rockets or a bomb load of 2,500 pounds (1,136 kg). The P-47 was designed around the advanced powerful Pratt & Whitney R-2800 Double Wasp engine which was also used by two U.S. Navy fighters, the Grumman F6F Hellcat and the Vought F4U Corsair. The Thunderbolt was effective as a short-to-medium range escort fighter in high-altitude air-to-air combat and ground attack in both the World War II European and Pacific theaters. The U.S. sent 203 P-47Ds to the Soviet Union.[44]

The Bell P-39 Airacobra was one of the principal American fighter aircraft in service when the United States entered World War II. The P-39 was used by the Soviet Air Force, and scored the highest number of individual kills attributed to any U.S. fighter type in the Eastern European theatre. A total of 4,719 P-39s were sent to the Soviet Union, accounting for more than one-third of all U.S. and UK-supplied fighter aircraft in the Soviet Military Air Forces (VVS).[45]

According to orders issued to the Lend Lease expeditor Major George Jordan: 'The President has directed that airplanes be delivered in accordance with protocol schedules by the most expeditious means. To implement these directives, the modification, equipment and movement of Russian planes have been given first priority, even over planes for U.S. Army Air Forces.'[46]

Roosevelt put the Soviets ahead of the British as well when 200 airplanes, originally intended for Britain's base in Singapore, were diverted to Russia. As a result of this diversion, Singapore fell to the Japanese on February 1942. Without British air support the Japanese were able to sink two British battleships costing the lives of more than eight hundred British sailors, including Admiral Sir Tom Phillips, and more than one hundred thousand British forces were forced to surrender. Roosevelt displayed his preference for the Soviets over East Asia when he stated "I would rather lose New Zealand, Australia, or anything else than have the Russian front collapse." [47]

According to the Russian historian Boris Vadimovich Sokolov, Lend-Lease had a crucial role in winning the war:

On the whole the following conclusion can be drawn: that without these Western shipments under Lend-Lease the Soviet Union not only would not have been able to win the Great Patriotic War, it would not have been able even to oppose the German invaders, since it could not itself produce sufficient quantities of arms and military equipment or adequate supplies of fuel and ammunition. The Soviet authorities were well aware of this dependency on Lend-Lease. Thus, Stalin told Harry Hopkins [FDR's emissary to Moscow in July 1941] that the U.S.S.R. could not match Germany's might as an occupier of Europe and its resources.[48]

Nikita Khrushchev, having served as a military commissar and intermediary between Stalin and his generals during the war, addressed directly the significance of Lend-lease aid in his memoirs:

I would like to express my candid opinion about Stalin's views on whether the Red Army and the Soviet Union could have coped with Nazi Germany and survived the war without aid from the United

States and Britain. First, I would like to tell about some remarks Stalin made and repeated several times when we were "discussing freely" among ourselves. He stated bluntly that if the United States had not helped us, we would not have won the war. If we had had to fight Nazi Germany one on one, we could not have stood up against Germany's pressure, and we would have lost the war. No one ever discussed this subject officially, and I don't think Stalin left any written evidence of his opinion, but I will state here that several times in conversations with me he noted that these were the actual circumstances. He never made a special point of holding a conversation on the subject, but when we were engaged in some kind of relaxed conversation, going over international questions of the past and present, and when we would return to the subject of the path we had traveled during the war, that is what he said. When I listened to his remarks, I was fully in agreement with him, and today I am even more so.[49]

There is absolutely no doubt that without British aid and the United States Lend-Lease aid to Russia, the Germans would have defeated the Russians and that would have been the end of Stalin and the communists.

Pearl Harbor

Pearl Harbor is another example of the disastrous consequences of politically motivated actions. Until May 1940, the Pacific Fleet was stationed on the west coast of the United States (primarily at San Diego). During the summer of that year, President Roosevelt ordered the fleet be moved to Pearl Harbor, Hawaii. Explanations for the move are hard to come by. There are some who believe that the move was designed to provoke a Japanese attack, which would provide a reason for the United States to get into the war and improve Roosevelt's chances for re-election. Others believed that the presence of the fleet in the Pacific would be a restraining influence on the Japanese. There were also some who believed that the fleet should never have been moved. One of those was Admiral Richardson.

James Otto Richardson (1878–1974) was an admiral in the United States Navy who served from 1902 to 1947. As Commander in Chief, United States Fleet (CINCUS), he protested against the redeployment of the Pacific portion of the fleet forward to Pearl Harbor, believing that a forward defense was neither practical nor useful, and that the Pacific Fleet would be the logical first target in the event of war with Japan, vulnerable to air and torpedo attacks. He was subsequently relieved of command in February 1941. His concerns were proven to be correct when the Japanese attacked Pearl Harbor ten months later.

At the time of his appointment, Admiral Richardson was particularly well suited for the post. Since his earliest days, after leaving Annapolis, he had made the study of Japanese warfare his life's work. He was beyond question the Navy's outstanding authority on Pacific naval warfare and Japanese strategy.[50]

Admiral Richardson explained the lack of security at Pearl Harbor. He described the congestion and the difficulty of operating ships in and out of its narrow entrance. He cited the inadequate facilities for fleet services, training, recreation, and housing. He also pointed out that the prolonged and indefinite stay away from the mainland during peacetime was bad for the morale of the men. But perhaps even more important than all these reasons, was the fact that the fleet at Pearl Harbor was not in a state of preparedness. If we went to war, it would have to return to the west coast to be outfitted, and that would involve a net loss of time.[51]

A Joint Congressional Committee for the Investigation of the Pearl Harbor Attack (JCC) was set up in the fall of 1945. In Admiral Richardson's testimony to the committee he provided his explanation for Roosevelt's decision to move the fleet: "The president stated that the fleet was retained in the Hawaiian area in order to exercise a restraining influence on the actions of Japan." Admiral Richardson doubted it would have that effect, for the Japanese military government knew full well that the U.S. Fleet in Hawaii was undermanned and unprepared for war.[52] In Richardson's words, "[I] could not help but detect that re-election political considerations, rather than long-range military considerations, were the controlling factor in the president's thinking."

In January 1941, Admiral Richardson was notified that he was being relieved of his command. Admiral Husband E. Kimmel was named to replace him, effective February 1. Richardson was "deeply disappointed in my detachment, yet," as he wrote later, "there was some feeling of prospective relief, for I had never liked to work with people whom I did not trust, and I did not trust Franklin D. Roosevelt." [53]

On his return to Washington, Richardson was directed to report to Secretary of the Navy Knox. When he called on Knox on March 24, he asked why he had been removed as CINCUS so peremptorily, after having served only 13 months of the usual 24-month tour of duty. "Why, Richardson," Knox responded, "When you were here in Washington last October, you hurt the President's feelings by what you said to him. You should realize that." [54]

Admiral Richardson was one of the foremost experts on Japan but rather than listen to him and heed his advice, Roosevelt fired him. Richardson's replacement Admiral Kimmel realized that, for strategic reasons, the Pacific Fleet did not belong at Pearl Harbor. He considered Richardson's arguments against holding the fleet there valid. Yet Kimmel realized he could not oppose the president on this issue and expect to retain his command. The Pacific fleet should have never been moved to Hawaii.

On October 30, 1940, Roosevelt made a campaign pledge to America that "Your boys are not going to be sent into any foreign wars." At the same time Roosevelt was pushing for legislation that would transfer war-making power from Congress to the President, and through the Lend-Lease program get America involved in the war.

These contradictory pronouncements were certainly intentional. Sometime later Ambassador Bullitt, a long-time intimate and adviser of Roosevelt's, as much as admitted that this equivocation had been deliberate. Roosevelt's "White House advisers," Bullitt wrote "persuaded him that if he told the truth he would lose the 1940 election. The president knew that war was coming to the American people. ... This was a low-water mark in presidential morality," Bullitt said, "but the president won the election." [55]

As far back as 1935, Ambassador Bullitt had reported to Secretary of State Cordell Hull that it is the "heartiest hope of the Soviet government that United States will become involved in war with Japan."[56] There is no doubt that Roosevelt and the War Department knew in advance that the Japanese were preparing for an attack in the Pacific. There were some who tried to persuade Roosevelt to change his policies and prevent a war with Japan, but Roosevelt ignored them.

Whether or not the repositioning of the Pacific Fleet was designed to provoke the Japanese into a first attack or not, there were additional warnings that the President's policies were leaving the Japanese with no choice but to attack the United States. U.S. Ambassador Grew in Japan kept Roosevelt fully advised of her precarious economic situation and urgent need for imports. Chief of Naval Operations (NCO) Stark had warned the president of the danger of imposing an oil embargo on Japan. Stark had "made it known to the State Department in no uncertain terms that in my opinion if Japan's oil were shut off, she would go to war." He did not mean "necessarily with us, but . . . if her economic life had been choked and throttled by inability to get oil, she would go somewhere and take it . . . and if I were a Jap, I would do the same." [57]

A message dated July 31, from the Japanese foreign minister in Tokyo to Japan's ambassador in Berlin expressed their concern over their desperate economic situation. A copy was sent to Kichisaburō Nomura, the Japanese Ambassador in Washington. It read in part: Commercial and economic relations between Japan and third countries, led by England and the United States, are gradually becoming so horribly strained that we cannot endure it much longer. Consequently, our Empire, to save its very life, must take measures to secure the raw materials of the South Seas. Our Empire must immediately take steps to break asunder this ever-strengthening chain of encirclement which is being woven under the guidance and with the participation of England and the United States, acting like a cunning dragon seemingly asleep. That is why we decided to obtain military bases in French Indo-China and to have our troops occupy that territory . . . and now Japanese-American relations are more rapidly than ever treading the evil road. [58]

It was General Marshall's position that, until U.S. power was sufficiently developed in the Philippines so we would "have something to back up our statements," the Japanese should not be antagonized unnecessarily. The United States should "make certain minor concessions which the Japanese could use in saving face," such as "a relaxation on oil restrictions or on similar trade restrictions." [59]

Marshall and Stark prepared a memorandum for the president, briefing him in some detail with respect to the Far East situation. One by one they pointed out the various reasons why the United States should not issue an ultimatum to Japan that might force her to take drastic action involving the United States in a Pacific war. It closed with a strong recommendation: "That no ultimatum be delivered to Japan." [60] Some of the reasons are provided below:

1. The U.S. fleet in the Pacific was inferior to the Japanese fleet and was not in a position to undertake an unlimited strategic offensive in the Western Pacific.

2. U.S. military forces in the Philippines were not yet strong enough. They were being reinforced, however, and it was expected that air and submarine strength would be built up by mid-December and that the air forces would reach their projected strength by February or March 1942.

3. British naval and air reinforcements were expected to reach Singapore by February or March.

Admiral Wilkinson made an appointment at noon on December 1, to go with Naval Intelligence Officer Arthur McCollum to see Chief of Naval Operations Stark. As McCollum later testified, "We knew that the Japanese fleet was ready for action. We knew that it had been called home, docked and extensively repaired and was looking for action." Also, the Japanese fleet had just changed its call signs and frequency allocations again after only a relatively short interval. This change in radio transmissions, when considered in conjunction with the various other clues, was one further indication that something was afoot.

Changing call signs, frequencies and codes typically points to a change in plans or preparation for some type of action. As in World War I, when the Germans changed their codes, the change of codes is always a sure sign of impending action.

Wilkinson, in subsequent testimony, said that "On the evidence available we had concluded…that the Japanese were contemplating an early attack, primarily directed at Thailand, Burma, and the Malay Peninsula." At the meeting with Stark, both Wilkinson and McCollum "urged that a dispatch of warning be sent to the fleet at that time." Stark assured them that such a dispatch had already been sent—on November 27—and that it had definitely included the phrase, "This is a war warning." [61]

On October 9, Washington cryptographers had deciphered a September 24 "berthing plan" intercept, instructing the Japanese consul in Hawaii to plot the location of ships in Pearl Harbor on a grid system and to notify Tokyo. However, the Pearl Harbor commanders were not notified. On December 3, Navy cryptanalysts in Washington decoded and translated a J-19 message more than two weeks old (November 15), sent from Tokyo to its consul in Hawaii. It read: "As relations between Japan and the United States are most critical, make your 'ships in harbor report' irregular, but at a rate of twice a week."[62]

Again, this information was not passed on to our commanders in Hawaii—not to General Short, who was responsible for the safety of the fleet while in port, and not to Admiral Kimmel, commander-in-chief of the Pacific Fleet based in Pearl Harbor. Thus the U.S. commanders in Hawaii remained ignorant of the fact that the Japanese consul in Honolulu was keeping a close watch on the ships of the U.S. fleet in Pearl Harbor.

Roosevelt and his war department knew well in advance that an attack was imminent. They knew if they kept pushing Japan, the Japanese would have no choice but to attack. Once they knew an attack was going to occur, they should have put all American military facilities on high alert. Sadly, this was not done. Ambassador Grew's repeated warnings that the Japanese would commit hara-kiri rather than submit to American dictation or starvation came true when the Japanese attacked Pearl Harbor.

As the *New York Times* reported on November 24, 1945, "Records of the State Department which were turned over today to the Congressional Committee Investigating Pearl Harbor, disclosed that the message sent by Joseph C. Grew, Ambassador to Japan, on Jan. 27, 1941, warning that the Japanese planned, in the event of trouble with the United States, to make a surprise attack on Pearl Harbor was based on information received by a member of the American Embassy staff in Tokyo from Dr. Ricardo Rivera Screiber, Peruvian Minister to Japan. The Minister was known as one with excellent Japanese sources."

Grew's account says "There is a lot of talk around town to the effect that the Japanese in case of a break with the United States, are planning to go all out in a surprise mass attack on Pearl Harbor. Of course, I informed our Government." Grew's report was provided to Admiral Harold R. Stark, Chief of Naval Operations, and Admiral Husband Kimmel, Commander-in-chief of the U.S. Pacific Fleet, but it was discounted by both.[63]

The attack on Pearl Harbor was a military strike by the Imperial Japanese Navy Air Service against the United States naval base at Pearl Harbor on the morning of December 7, 1941. The attack led to the United States' entry into World War II. Japan intended the attack as a preventive action to keep the U.S. Pacific Fleet from interfering with its planned military actions in Southeast Asia against overseas territories of the United Kingdom, the Netherlands, and the United States.

As a result of poor decisions, flagrant disregard of critical information, and the political ambitions and dictatorial power and ego of President Roosevelt, the United States had been attacked. All eight U.S. Navy battleships were damaged, with four sunk. All but the USS Arizona were later raised, and six were returned to service and went on to fight in the war. The Japanese also sank or damaged three cruisers, and three destroyers. One hundred sixty-nine U.S. aircraft were destroyed and one hundred and fifty-nine aircraft were damaged; 2,403 Americans were killed and 1,178 others were wounded.

Based on all the evidence there can be only one conclusion, President Roosevelt is to blame for the disastrous attack on Pearl Harbor. Percy L. Greaves in his book *Pearl Harbor: The Seeds and Fruits of Infamy* summarizes this conclusion as follows:

It must be said also that the evidence revealed in the course of the several investigations leads to the conclusion that the ultimate responsibility for the catastrophe inflicted on the U.S. Fleet at

Pearl Harbor on December 7, 1941, must rest on the shoulders of President Roosevelt, to whom the Constitution assigns authority as Commander in Chief of the Army and Navy and the responsibility to preserve, protect and defend the Constitution of the United States. It is now evident that the stage was set for a Japanese attack on U.S. territory by President Roosevelt's decisions and actions. He was responsible for squeezing the Japanese economically until they were forced to try to use force to seize the resources they needed and to prevent the U.S. Fleet from trying to stop them. It was thanks to Roosevelt's decisions and actions that an unwarned, ill-equipped, and poorly prepared Fleet remained stationed far from the shores of continental United States, at a base recognized by his military advisers as indefensible and vulnerable to attack. Given that situation, it is not strange that the Fleet was surprised by the attack of Japanese torpedo planes and bombers that fateful Sunday morning, December 7, 1941. And then when the extent of the damage was known, it was Roosevelt who orchestrated a cover-up to make Admiral Kimmel and General Short scapegoats and to conceal any negligence on the part of the administration.[64]

A similar conclusion is reached by an objective British historian, Captain Russell Grenfell, in his book *Main Fleet to Singapore*:

No reasonably informed person can now believe that Japan made a villainous, unexpected attack on the United States. An attack was not only fully expected but was actually desired. It is beyond doubt that President Roosevelt wanted to get his country into the war, but for political reasons was most anxious to ensure that the first act of hostility came from the other side; for which reason he caused increasing pressure to be put on the Japanese, to a point that no self-respecting nation could endure without resort to arms. As Mr. Oliver Lyttelton, then British Minister of Production, said in 1944, "Japan was provoked into attacking America at Pearl Harbor. It is a travesty of history to say that America was forced into the war."

As General Wedemeyer points out, President Roosevelt had ample time to broadcast a warning. Conjecturally, such a warning might even have caused the Japanese to call off their surprise attack. In any event, we would not have permitted 2,403 Americans to die at Hawaii without an opportunity to fight back. [65]

The official war between the United States and Germany began with the German Declaration of War with the United States on December 11, 1941. The German Charge d'Affaires, Dr. Hans Thomsen, and the First Secretary of the German Embassy, Mr. von Strempel, called at the State Department at 8:00 A.M. on December 11, 1941. The Secretary, otherwise engaged, directed that they be received by the Chief of the European Division of the State Department, Mr. Ray Atherton. Mr. Atherton received the German representatives at 9:30 A.M. The German representatives handed to Mr. Atherton a copy of a note that is being delivered this morning, December 11, to the American Charge d'Affaires in Berlin. Dr. Thomsen said that Germany considers herself in a state of war with the United States.

The text of the note which the German representatives handed to Mr. Ray Atherton, Chief of the European

Division of the State Department, at 9:30 A.M., December 11, the original of which had been delivered the morning of December 11 to the American Charge d'Affaires in Berlin, follows:

The Government of the United States having violated in the most flagrant manner and in ever increasing measure all rules of neutrality in favor of the adversaries of Germany and having continually been guilty of the most severe provocations toward Germany ever since the outbreak of the European war, provoked by the British declaration of war against Germany on September 3, 1939, has finally resorted to open military acts of aggression.

On September 11, 1941, the President of the United States publicly declared that he had ordered the American Navy and Air Force to shoot on sight at any German war vessel. In his speech of October 27, 1941, he once more expressly affirmed that this order was in force. Acting under this order, vessels of the American Navy, since early September 1941, have systematically attacked German naval forces. Thus, American destroyers, as for instance the Greer, the Kearney and the Reuben James, have opened fire on German sub-marines according to plan. The Secretary of the American Navy, Mr. Knox, himself confirmed that-American destroyers attacked German submarines.

Furthermore, the naval forces of the United States, under order of their Government and contrary to international law have treated and seized German merchant vessels on the high seas as enemy ships. The German Government therefore establishes the following facts:

Although Germany on her part has strictly adhered to the rules of international law in her relations with the United States during every period of the present war, the Government of the United States from initial violations of neutrality has finally proceeded to open acts of war against Germany. The Government of the United States has thereby virtually created a state of war.

The German Government, consequently, discontinues diplomatic relations with the United States of America and declares that under these circumstances brought about by President Roosevelt, Germany too, as from today, considers herself as being in a state of war with the United States of America.[66]

The Roosevelt administration's enthusiasm for the Russians began immediately upon taking office. One of the first acts of the new Roosevelt administration was to grant diplomatic recognition of the Soviet Union. This despite the Soviets stated hatred of capitalist nations and their goal of a world socialist revolution. Roosevelt named William C. Bullitt to be the first U.S. ambassador to the U.S.S.R. Bullitt considered communism a harbinger for the world and was an enthusiastic proponent of the Soviet system.

On November 16, 1933, the United States recognized the government of the Union of Soviet Socialist Republics (U.S.S.R). The professed purpose of recognition was so "that our nations henceforth may cooperate for their mutual benefit and for the preservation of the peace of the world." The peace of the world didn't last long. Roosevelt got the United States into the war with Germany and Japan for political reasons and so he could save his communist comrades in the Soviet Union and China.

Once Roosevelt got America into the war, he threw his full support behind Russia. The President spelled out his plan in a memorandum dated April 8, 1942, in which he wrote: "Western Europe is favored as the theater in which to stage the first major offensive by the United States and Great Britain. Only there could their combined land and air resources be fully developed and the maximum support given to Russia." [67]

From the start of the war Stalin was insisting upon a second front. The communists even organized mass demonstrations in London demanding a 'Second Front Now'. Stalin kept insisting that the Allies start a second front and for Roosevelt to keep his promise of a major invasion of France in the spring of 1944. This guaranteed that the Balkans and central Europe would fall to the Soviets and be under the control of the Red Army. Following Stalin's orders General Marshall and Roosevelt refused any help or assistance in operations in the Mediterranean or Italy.

In most wars there are always tactical and strategic errors, mistakes and mismanagement, and bad decisions. War is a chaotic and ugly business. These facts certainly apply to the United States involvement in World War II. The American soldier's bravery and heroism is beyond compare. Their suffering and sacrifice were horrific, their resilience truly amazing. The management of the war by the War Department and the politicians was a different story. Examples of misguided tactical decisions are many, some more disastrous than others, but the lessons learned should not be forgotten.

The Falaise Pocket or Falaise Gap (August 1944) was the decisive engagement of the Battle of Normandy in the Second World War. A pocket was formed around

Falaise, Calvados, in which the German Army Group B, with the 7th Army and the Fifth Panzer Army were encircled by the Western Allies.

The Third Army advance from the south was making good progress. Alençon was captured and German Field Marshall von Kluge was forced to commit troops he had been gathering for a counter-attack. The next day, the 5th US Armored Division of the XV US Corps advanced 35 mi (56 km) and reached positions overlooking Argentan. On August 13th, Bradley over-ruled orders by Patton for a further push northward towards Falaise by the 5th Armored Division. Bradley instead ordered the XV Corps to "concentrate for operations in another direction". The US troops near Argentan were ordered to withdraw, which ended the pincer movement by the XV Corps. Patton objected but complied, which left an exit for the German forces in the Falaise Pocket.

The international army boundary arbitrarily divided the British and American battlefields just beyond Argentan, on the Falaise side of it. Patton's troops, who thought they had the mission of closing the gap, took Argentan in their stride and crossed the international boundary without stopping. Montgomery, who was still nominally in charge of all ground forces, now chose to exercise his authority and ordered Patton back to his side of the international boundary line. ... For ten days, however, the beaten but still coherently organized German Army retreated through the Falaise gap. [68]

If Patton had been allowed to close the gap at Falaise it could have resulted in the surrender of the Third Reich. General Bradley's own historian Colonel Ralph Ingersoll wrote, "The failure to close the Argentan-Falaise gap was the loss of the greatest single opportunity of the war." [69]

General Bradley inexplicably supported Montgomery and halted Patton. By the time Montgomery closed the gap, thousands of German commanders and troops, along with artillery and tanks, had escaped through the Falaise Gap. As a result of the failure to close the Falaise gap, the Germans had the manpower and equipment that was critical to the Battle of the Bulge.

The Hurtgen Forest campaign started on September 12, 1944, when the veteran 9th Infantry Division attacked the southern end of the forest in an attempt to move through a passage known as the Monschau Corridor. Although it is little remembered today, the battle for the Hurtgen Forest was one of the worst defeats ever suffered by the U.S. Army.

Top officers responsible for the fiasco – Ike Eisenhower, Omar Bradley, Courtney Hodges and Lawton Collins, among them – went on to be honored in retirement. More important, given the experience of the 9th Division during the opening phase of the battle, the larger question is why senior American leaders such as Generals Courtney Hodges, Omar Bradley and Dwight D. Eisenhower chose in November 1944, to send division after division into the dark and foreboding woods right until the start of the German Ardennes offensive that December. In three months of combat operations, the Americans sustained almost 33,000 casualties but accomplished almost nothing tactically or operationally in the process.

An exception to the rule of generals covering up their mistakes was James Gavin, commander of the 82nd Airborne, who always jumped into combat with his men and carried the enlisted man's weapon, the M-1 Garand. He broke ranks to admit: "For us, the Hurtgen was one of the most costly, most unproductive, and most ill-advised battles that our army has ever fought." [70]

These are just two examples of the many terrible mistakes by General Eisenhower. It is hard to believe that

Eisenhower was just a clueless, error prone commander. With a pro-soviet War Department, it is no wonder that he gave the Soviets preferential treatment over his own American forces. In what may have been Eisenhower's greatest blunder, he stopped Patton from taking Berlin, Vienna and Prague. Some consider this one of the greatest blunders in political and military history.

Stalin was totally against any Allied attacks from Italy into Austria and Germany, and effectively stopped any invasion into the Balkans from the Adriatic or the Aegean Seas. The US decision to abandon Italy in favor of Northern France was done at Stalin's command to ensure that Central and Eastern Europe remained open for a future Soviet invasion.

Roosevelt had already sealed the fate of Eastern Europe long before the Soviet Red Army had even fought its way out of Russia. As recounted by Cardinal Spellman in a conversation with Roosevelt, "The European people will simply have to endure Russian domination in the hope that in ten to twenty years they be able to live well with the Russians." Roosevelt had said this while the Red Army was still fighting inside Russia. In other words, he knew he was going to hand over Eastern Europe to Stalin and didn't give a damn about the fate of the European people.

In another disgraceful act, Roosevelt and Churchill sacrificed Singapore and the Philippines to the Soviets. While Stalin was ordering Churchill and Roosevelt to establish a second front as soon as possible, thousands of Americans and Filipinos were struggling for their lives on the Bataan death march and trying to hang on at Corregidor. The US had pledged to protect the Philippines and had failed miserably. Ten thousand American and Filipino troops were killed at Bataan and twenty thousand were wounded.

The loss of the Philippines occurred as General MacArthur was pleading for supplies and aircraft, "just three planes so I can see. You can't fight them if you can't see them. I am now blind." [71] The only thing General MacArthur received from Washington were empty promises as the vital supplies, aircraft, and weapons he needed were diverted to the Soviet Union.

Reinvading Europe through both northern France (Operation Overlord) and southern France (Operation Anvil), rather than pressing on from the already established Allied front and bases in Italy, and expanding operations from the Adriatic and Aegean Seas into south central Europe, as Churchill desperately and repeatedly proposed, left Eastern and Central Europe wide open to the Soviet Red Army.

As General Mark Clark noted, "The weakening of the campaign in Italy in order to invade Southern France instead of pushing on into the Balkan's was one of the outstanding political mistakes of the war."

Just like Roosevelt and Truman, Eisenhower was bamboozled by the Russians. It is not a misstatement to say that he was taking orders from the Russians. Eisenhower showed his capitulation to the Russians many times. In one example, Patton and the Third Army were poised to take Prague. Eisenhower was told by General Antonov, the Red Army Chief of Staff, not to move forces into Prague. Upon receiving his orders from the Russian Chief of Staff, Eisenhower immediately halted the Third Army's advance. He ordered General Bradley to find Patton wherever he was and tell him that under no circumstances was he to go in force beyond the Budweis-Pilsen-Karlsbad line. Moreover, the city of Prague was not to be touched.

Patton had previously called General Bradley and told him Prague was ripe for the picking and asked, "Is this stop line through Pilsen really mandatory? Can't you just let me go to into Prague? For God's sake, Brad, those patriots in the city need our help! We have no time to lose!" [72]

Averell Harriman, who served as Ambassador to the Soviet Union, was apparently one of the few in the Roosevelt administration who understood the Soviets and recognized the conflict between Bolshevism and the Western democracies. He told Patton that Stalin had paid the Third Army the highest compliment by saying in the presence of the Red Army Chief of Staff, "The Red Army could not have conceived and certainly could not have executed the advance made by the Third Army across France."

But he also warned Patton that Stalin was "a strong ruthless revolutionist, and therefore a very potential threat to future world conditions." He described the discipline in the Red Army as "the most rigid and ruthless he had ever seen" and its officer caste as the "new nobility." [73]

There were what appeared to be multiple attempts on General Patton's life, and it was well known that he was feared and hated by the Nazis, the Soviets, and American politicians and people in the military.

American forces could have easily taken Berlin, Vienna and Prague. But the spineless Eisenhower on orders from his communist superiors did not give the order to advance; he gave the order to stop. General Patton's Third Army and General Simpson's Ninth Army were constantly being stopped by the Roosevelt War Department.

General Patton summed up his frustration with weak American policy of appeasement towards the Soviets in a phone conversation with General McNarney. "Hell, what do you care what those Goddamn Russians think? We are going to have fight them sooner or later; within the next generation. Why not do it now while our Army is intact and the damn Russians can have their hind end kicked back to Russia in three months?" [74]

Japan had just surrendered to the Allies, ending World War II, but Stalin, who had only declared war on Japan seven days before its capitulation, was eager to seize territory Roosevelt and Churchill had promised to the Soviet Union. He sent troops to occupy the southern Kuril Islands, which Russia had acknowledged as Japanese territory in 1855. In 1947, Russian ships arrived and took all the Japanese away. They were allowed to pack one bag and given 24 hours to get on board.

Russia was never our ally, despite the best efforts of Roosevelt to make it look like they were. The Russians made a deal with the Germans so they didn't have to fight. Then the Germans reneged on the deal and attacked them. They had no choice but to fight the Germans. They had to fight for their survival, not because they wanted to help the West. Before, during, and after the war, the Soviets regarded the Western nations as the enemy – the capitalist imperialists.

Everyone but the clueless and the communists knew that the Soviets were our enemy. The people in power knew. They were either communists or believed in world socialism and they in turn, duped the clueless into believing that the Russians were our friends.

The fact is that the US didn't need the Soviet Red Army to defeat Germany and Japan. We should have let the Germans defeat the Soviets then two evil empires could have been destroyed.

Soviet Atrocities

The atrocities committed by Stalin fill volumes. As stated earlier, the world knew Stalin, yet the communist faithful believed that the end justifies the means and that torturing and killing non-believers is an acceptable practice in achieving their goal of a global socialist utopia. The horrific nature of warfare on the Eastern Front was magnified by the rape, robbery, and murder directed at the local civilian population by the advancing Red Army.[75]

Hitler and the Germans didn't treat the Russians any worse than Stalin and the NKVD treated their own people. Stalin's total disregard for human life applied to his own people and troops. Stalin's brutal commander Zhukov, ordered commanders to 'Make it clear to all troops that all the families of those who surrender to the enemy will be shot and they themselves will be shot upon return from prison.'

Russian POWs were considered traitors of the Motherland because they failed to kill themselves. Stalin had no feelings for civilians either, on hearing that the Germans had forced 'old men and women, mother and children 'forward as human shields or as emissaries to demand surrender, he sent orders that they were to be shot down.[76]

Blocking groups were set up in each army to gun down those who retreated. Punishment battalions were strengthened with 30,000 Gulag prisoners. The deaths of the Gulag prisoners in 1942 alone amounted to 352,560, a quarter of its whole population. Many of the Soviet soldiers could not take the psychological strain of battle. During the Stalingrad campaign alone, a total of 13,000 Soviet soldiers were executed for cowardice or desertion.[77]

The atrocities committed by the Soviets were so great the Germans would kill themselves rather than be taken by the Red Army. 'Russian soldiers were raping every

German female from eight to eighty', observed Soviet war correspondent Natalya Gesse.

Patton and Eisenhower disagreed on many issues, both political and military. In one of the saddest chapters in American and British history, the Russian repatriation known as Operation Keelhaul, Patton strongly opposed repatriation, while Eisenhower not only endorsed it, he brutally enforced it.

Julius Epstein, a journalist and scholar, and a Research Associate at the Hoover Institution on War, Revolution and Peace, revealed details of Operation Keelhaul, the forced repatriation at the end of World War II of four million Soviet citizens, expatriated White Russians who had emigrated from Russia after the Bolshevik Revolution, and other Eastern Europeans to the Soviet Union and countries within its sphere of influence after 1945. Most were condemned to lengthy prison terms, some in the gulag, and many were executed, including some who were summarily executed within earshot of British and American troops the moment that they were handed over to the Soviets.[78]

Its victims were thousands of refugees, both soldiers and civilians fleeing to the West from the successful advance of the Red armies through Eastern Europe. They were hoping to escape Communist tyranny and find asylum, but instead they were all collected by the Allied armies and forcibly repatriated into the anxious arms of the Soviets.

The victims of Operation Keelhaul included not only soldiers wearing German uniforms, but also civilians, as the fate of the Cossacks illustrates. When the German forces were slowly pushed out of Russia, not only did the Cossack troops withdraw, but large numbers from the Cossack nation went with them. The trek was long and arduous, but at the end of the war nearly 30,000

Cossacks - families, with many women, children, and old men - had put themselves under the protection of the 11th British Armored Division near Leinz, Austria. They had been joined by many old Cossack émigrés who had left Russia during the Civil Wars from 1917 to 1920 and had since lived in Yugoslavia or Germany.

Over 2000 Cossack officers, including the very aged Peter Krasnov, who had led the White armies allied with the British during the Russian Civil War but had not been in Russia since, boarded a convoy of over 75 vehicles escorted by 25 Bren gun carriers, and then were taken, not as they had been told to a conference, but to the waiting Soviets at Judenburg. Krasnov and his associates, like Vlasov, were subsequently hanged.

Back at Leinz, word of the fate of their officers and of the XV Corps had filtered back to the remaining Cossacks, who organized a passive resistance in which the soldiers and cadets would link arms and form a protective chain around the older men, women, and children. That is what they did at dawn on June 1st, when the camps were surrounded by British Bren gun carriers and armed troops. At a signal, the troops advanced into the crowds and began clubbing the Cossacks with rifle butts and batons. Those who tried to run away were shot in the feet and legs. The victims were thrown onto a convoy of waiting trucks, which took them to the nearby rail road siding. As each cattle-car was filled, it was bound shut with barbed wire and another car was loaded.

Many tried to commit suicide along the banks of the Drava River. One woman, who was dragged out downstream and revived, turned out to be a doctor who had earlier killed her daughter and mother with overdoses of morphine rather than let them suffer repatriation. Her second attempt at suicide succeeded. Isolated British troops, fearing for their lives in the melee, opened fire.

The Bren gun carriers advanced to compress the crowds, and one woman threw her baby and then herself under the tracks to be crushed. Two Cossack men approached a British officer and addressed him in Russian. As the officer asked his interpreter for a translation, both men slit their own throats and slumped to the ground, twitching and dying. "Our blood is on you and your children," was the translation of their statement. An engineer from Novocherkassk shot his twelve-year old son, his one-year old daughter, his wife, and then himself. Hundreds killed themselves in various fashions.

As the dust settled on defeated Germany, the Allied armies started the huge task of herding together all the prisoners of war and refugees and concentrating them in Displaced Persons (DP) camps. Many had in their possession Allied leaflets dropped from the air which branded as a lie the Nazi charges that prisoners would be shipped to Russia. Nevertheless, special repatriation teams of Allied and Soviet officials went through the camps questioning and screening in order to sort out all who might have been residents of the Soviet Union or the Eastern European countries. Those to be repatriated were sent to special camps which were policed by British and American troops under the supervision of Soviet officials, who insured that any anti-Communist propaganda or activity was suppressed.

In short, the Allied armies tracked down everyone who could conceivably be construed as a Russian or Eastern European citizen - men, women, and children, soldiers and civilians, those who had fought with Germany and those who had fought against Germany, collected them together and brutally handed them over to Stalin and his minions. It is estimated that between two to five million victims were involved.

The excuse of those who participated in and executed Operation Keelhaul was that they were "acting under orders," that forced repatriation was required by the Yalta Agreement. However, as Epstein conclusively demonstrates, the Yalta Agreements; while calling for a system of repatriation; said absolutely nothing about the use of force, and furthermore, Operation Keelhaul was already in full swing in June 1944, eight months prior to Yalta.[79]

Welch and Huxley-Blythe, in their previous accounts, have asserted that the individual bearing the primary responsibility for originating and implementing Operation Keelhaul was the commander of SHAEF, General Eisenhower. But Eisenhower was just following orders from the head communists, Stalin, President Roosevelt, and his co-president Harry Hopkins.

The reason that the responsibility for Operation Keelhaul remains so obscure is that all the relevant documents still remain locked up and inaccessible. Three volumes of records; entitled "Forcible' Repatriation of Displaced Soviet Citizens-Operation Keelhaul," were classified Top Secret by the U.S. Army on September 18, 1948, and bear the secret file number 383.7-14.1. Other documents are being held under wraps in the UNRRA Archives by the U.N. Secretariat and in the British Archives by the British Government. Epstein, who earlier was instrumental in uncovering the truth about the Katyn Forest massacre, has been attempting for 20 years, since 1954, to get the veil of secrecy removed from the Keelhaul documents. So far, his efforts, including a suit under the Freedom of Information Act of 1966, have proven fruitless.

Not only were the Allied governments able to perpetrate the crime, but afterwards, they were able to impose what Harry Elmer Barnes has appropriately called an "historical blackout" so effective that it lasted for nearly 30 years.[80]

The Katyn massacre, in which Soviet functionaries executed Polish military officers and secretly dumped their bodies into mass graves, is further evidence that Roosevelt was a communist. In one of the more blatant examples of his support of Stalin, when a report by a respected naval officer about the murder of thousands of Polish soldiers and civilians implicated the Soviets, Roosevelt suppressed the report and banished the author.

The murders were carried out by the Soviet NKVD (The People's Commissariat for Internal Affairs). The 1940 Katyn massacre had been carried out at the order of Roosevelt's comrade Stalin. Of course, 'Uncle Joe' and the Soviets blamed the Nazis and denied any role in the killings.

The NKVD undertook mass extrajudicial executions of untold numbers of citizens and conceived, populated and administered the Gulag system of forced labor camps. Their agents were responsible for the repression of the Kulaks and the mass deportations of entire nationalities to uninhabited regions of the country. They oversaw the protection of Soviet borders and espionage (which included political assassinations), and enforced Soviet policy in communist movements and puppet governments in other countries, most notably the repression and massacres in Poland.

How could FDR put his trust in Stalin's word? As historian Fraser Harbutt reminds us by the time the 1945 Yalta conference had begun, the Poles had endured the Red Army's invasion and ruthless occupation of 1939-41; the forcible deportation of 1.5 million of their citizens to the Soviet Union, where thousands died in labor camps, and the brutal executions of the Katyn massacre.

Convinced that he needed a Polish settlement to secure domestic support for his dream of a United Nations, Roosevelt instructed his aides to delete the offending provision for election observers. No man with any moral fiber would continue to provide cover for such atrocities.

China and Korea

As a result of the weakness, timidity, and capitulation displayed by the Roosevelt administration toward Stalin, and with further assistance by the Truman administration, the communists continued their advance in China and Korea.

The civil war between the Chinese Communist Party (CCP) and the Nationalist Party, or Kuomintang (KMT), broke out immediately following World War II and had been preceded by on and off conflict between the two sides since the 1920's. After the Japanese invaded Manchuria in 1931, the Government of the Republic of China (ROC) faced the triple threat of Japanese invasion, Communist uprising, and warlord insurrections.

The Russians had a major impact on the Communist Party of China. It was a large number of Soviet advisors that helped transform a loose collection of militant intellectuals into the Chinese Communist Party. Comintern officials were present when the Chinese Communists held their founding congress in July 1921.[81] The Soviets sent money, munitions, and spies to support the Chinese Communist Party. Without their support the Chinese Communist Party would have certainly failed.

Handing over China to the communists began with Roosevelt's hideous secret Far Eastern Agreement signed at Yalta on February 11, 1945. This secret agreement in effect handed Mongolia, Manchuria, and the Kuril Islands over to Stalin.

As President Hoover points out, "Despite all the awards and gifts to Stalin in this Far Eastern Agreement, he did not join the war against Japan until after she was in fact defeated by the use of the atomic bomb. However, he held on to all the concessions in the Far East Agreement. The text of this agreement was not furnished to Chiang Kai-shek for some months, nor to all the members of the Yalta Conference, nor was it given to the American people until February 11, 1946, a year after the agreement was signed." [82]

General Wedemeyer, who was named chief of staff in the Allied command structure to Generalissimo Chiang Kai-shek, and assumed command of the newly established China Theater of Operations, recommended increased U.S. support of the Nationalist government, and warned of an imminent Communist triumph in the absence of that support. Contrary to Wedemeyer's recommendations, the Truman administration opted for a policy aimed at unifying China by reconciling the contending factions. To implement this policy, President Truman sent recently retired General Marshall to China as ambassador with the mission of bringing the Nationalist and Communist Parties together in a coalition government and integrating their armed forces. When these efforts failed at the end of 1946, armed conflict resumed with heightened intensity. Wedemeyer was relieved of his Chinese duties in September 1946, and assigned stateside to command the Second U.S. Army. Wedemeyer concluded that indecisive and misguided

U.S. policy had helped push China over the brink and allowed Mao and the Communists to take power.[83]

President Chiang Kai-shek and the Nationalists went on to develop the Republic of China on Taiwan, a spectacularly free and successful economy and an increasingly free and stable political democracy. General Wedemeyer often contrasted this achievement with Mao's totalitarian Communist regime on the mainland.

The cease fire agreement between the Nationalists and the Communists paralyzed Chiang Kai-shek and benefited Mao. Chiang Kai-shek had loyally ceased all military action while Mao continued his guerilla warfare. The agreement further benefited the communists who needed time to train a new army of over a million men. In May 1946, Stalin and Mao entered into an agreement by which 5,000 Russians were to train Mao's armies in the use of their newly acquired captured Japanese weapons, and American Lend-Lease arms, which had been supplied to Mao. The cease fire and later the tragic mistake by General Marshall to force a coalition government on Chiang Kai-shek would lead to victory for the communists.

Chiang Kai-shek and the Nationalists were not perfect, but they were far better than Mao and the Communists. Marshall admitted that it was a mistake to use the word "coalition" for the form of government the Truman administration hoped the Chinese could agree upon.[84]

Minnesota Republican Walter H. Judd suspected that the directive under which Marshall operated while in China was purposefully flawed. "It completely reversed America's traditional foreign policy of many years without anybody's knowing it."

The directive included a cessation of hostilities be arranged between the armies of the National Government and the Chinese Communists and other dissident Chinese armed forces, and that the Government be broadened to include other political elements in the country. Marshall edited and approved this directive.

The directive, Judd asserted, not only was a key reason Chiang did not believe the United States would support him, thus making it impossible for him to seek reforms, but it also encouraged the Communists. He continued, "I think that directive, in essence, lost World War II for us." Judd twice asked Marshall to tell him who in the State Department's Far Eastern Division had written the directive, but Marshall did not respond.[85] All he could do was repeat the Roosevelt administrations slogan that Mao was an agrarian reformer.

The American press had now turned against the Nationalist regime, describing it as dictatorial, incompetent, corrupt and nepotistic. Newspapers accused it of refusing to fight the Japanese and of indifference towards the Chinese people, especially during the major famine in Honan the year before. The *New York Times* claimed that support for the Nationalists made America 'acquiesce in an unenlightened cold-hearted autocratic regime'. Influential writers, such as Theodore White, vilified Chiang Kai-shek and contrasted him unfavorably with the Communists. In the era of New Deal liberalism, many State Department officials agreed.[86]

Communist supporters such as American journalist Edgar Snow had managed to persuade readers in the United States that Mao's forces were fighting hard while the corrupt Nationalists were doing little, when in fact the opposite was true. Edgar Snow once described Mao and the Chinese communists as a progressive force who desired a democratic free China.

The support of Mao and the communists continued in the Truman administration. Truman himself had a violent animosity towards Chiang Kai-shek. Truman's sacrifice of China to the communists by "insistence of his left-wing advisors and his appointment of General Marshall to execute their will" was a disgraceful act. A young veteran of the war in the Pacific, Congressman John F. Kennedy stated later at an address in Salem, Massachusetts: "This is a tragic story of China whose freedom we once fought to preserve. What our young men had saved, our diplomats and our President have frittered away."

General MacArthur expanded on what the young John F. Kennedy had said. 'The failure of those in authority to implement existing United States policy brought about the downfall of an ally and jeopardized the very security of our nation. We have seen the growth of a communist enemy where we once had a staunch ally. We have watched communist imperialism spread its influence throughout the world. We have seen thousands of our young men vainly sacrifice their lives in blind pursuit of sterile policies of appeasement and ignorance of history and of this enemy.'[87]

The failure to stop the Communists from taking control of China lead directly to the Korean War, where again, communist forces in the United States government sabotaged General MacArthur's plan to defeat the Chinese Communists and re-unify Korea.

After the secret deal with Stalin that handed Manchuria over to the Russians, they rapidly advanced south into North Korea. Clueless about Russian intentions the Truman administration appeared surprised by the Russian advance and came up with plan that would appease the Russians by dividing Korea into two parts. The northern half would fall under the Russian sphere of influence, while the southern half would fall under the American sphere of influence.

The arbitrary line at the 38th parallel divided what was once a unified nation. As a result of the partition, two opposite states emerged on the Korean peninsula. In the north, the Russians organized the Democratic People's Republic under the communist leader Kim Il Sung. In the south the Republic of Korea was formed under the leadership of Syngman Rhee. The Korean War began on June 25, 1950, when the North invaded the South in an unprovoked attack. The fighting ended on July 27, 1953, when an armistice was signed.

The case of the Chinese communists involved two major failures. The first was the failure of the United States of America to support the Chinese Nationalists led by Generalissimo Chiang Kai-shek in the civil war against the Chinese Communists. The second was the capitulation by the Americans during the Korean War. In China, the Chinese Nationalists were pushing the communists back. The clueless leaders of the United States referred to the Chinese communists as 'agrarian reformers', and instead of arming and supporting the Nationalists, pushed for an armistice. While the United States displayed weakness and indecision, and did nothing, the Soviet communists reinforced the Chinese communist armies. This allowed the Chinese communists to defeat the Nationalists.

As General MacArthur, Supreme Commander of Allied Forces in the Pacific noted, 'The decision to withhold previously pledged American support was one of the greatest mistakes ever made in our history.'

Senator Thomas Dodd of Connecticut stated in a speech on the senate floor: 'In a decision for which we as a nation can truly be held responsible, the opportunity to crush the aggressive power of Communist China at its outset was lost by default and America proceeded upon a policy of vacillation and retreat from victory which, with each passing year, brings its harvest of shame and defeat.'

General MacArthur had a plan that would have neutralized China from waging future war and save Asia from engulfment utilizing only a small part of the United States overall military potential. As General MacArthur correctly stated, 'Red China lacks the industrial capacity to adequately provide many critical items essential to the conduct of modern war. He lacks at this time the manufacturing and those raw materials needed to produce, maintain, and operate even moderate air and naval power, and he cannot provide the essentials for successful ground operations, such as tanks, heavy artillery, and other refinements science has introduced into the conduct of military campaigns.' [88]

China was not ready to risk a war with the United States, and if only the non-communist US leaders would have had a backbone, Korea would be unified today. As General MacArthur points out from an official document by the Chinese General Lin Piao: 'I would have never have made the attack and risked my men and military reputation if I had not been assured that Washington would restrain General MacArthur from taking adequate retaliatory measures against my lines of supply and communication.' [89]

In the Korean War, General MacArthur led a bold and brilliant campaign and defeated the North Koreans bringing the Korean War to a practical end. The Chinese then moved elements of Chinese communist forces across the Yalu River into North Korea and massed a large concentration of reinforcing divisions and supplies behind the privileged sanctuary of the adjacent Manchurian border. General MacArthur wanted to destroy the Yalu River bridges and cut the lines of communication between Manchuria and North Korea.

After ordering the bombing of the Yalu bridges an immediate dispatch was delivered from Secretary Marshall countermanding his order and directing him to "postpone all bombing of targets within five miles of the Manchurian border. MacArthur's reaction is as follows: 'It seemed to me incredible that protection should be extended to the enemy. It would be impossible to exaggerate my astonishment.'[90] Such blatant appeasement to the enemy is truly astonishing.

Due to timidity, weakness and appeasement, General MacArthur was stopped from bombing the Yalu River bridges by politicians in the United States and the United Nations. As General MacArthur stated, 'the order not to bomb the Yalu bridges was the most indefensible and ill-conceived decisions ever forced on a field commander in the nation's history.'

Displaying either incredible ignorance and a total lack of leadership, or even worse, complicity with Soviet and Chinese communists, President Truman allowed Asia to be defeated by communism, resulting in the enslavement of millions of formerly free people. General MacArthur described the outcome as follows, 'The abandonment of the pledged commitments of the United States and the United Nations to restore to the people of Korea a nation, which was unified and free, in whose solemn declaration the people of Asia had placed such trust and faith, was a catastrophic blow to the hopes of the free world. Its disastrous consequences were reflected throughout Asia. The Chinese communists were promptly accepted as the military colossus of the East. Korea was left ravished and divided. Indochina was partitioned by the sword.' [91]

There were some who recognized the disastrous policies of Roosevelt and Truman. Congressman Dorn, a member of a Congressional committee investigating conditions in the Far East stated the following:

The North Korean attack and subsequent entrance of Red China into the war was a God given opportunity for the United States to correct with little cost the tragic mistakes of Yalta and Potsdam. Red China's only armies were ground to pieces in North Korea. The Russians were recuperating from World War II and did not have nuclear weapons in mass production.

Some day we will have to fight Red China on her terms at a time of her choosing. She will have atomic power backed by the entire Eurasian land mass. This issue could have been resolved forever in our favor in 1951 had those of us in Washington had the foresight to give MacArthur the green light in Asia. This great General could have secured the peace and could have assured the ascendency of the Western democratic world. MacArthur was right and many of us here in Washington, in London, and in the United Nations were wrong.

To all the doubters of the courageous people who exposed the treason of the Roosevelt and Truman administrations, it seems that a question you may want to ask is, why did they want to silence General Patton and General McArthur?

As the *Encyclopedia of Military History* states in its introduction to World War II and leadership: "In military leadership we believe that one man – Douglas MacArthur – may have risen to join the thin ranks of the great captains of history." In this case, they mean in the history of warfare dating back to 3500 B.C. and 3000 B.C. in Mesopotamia and Egypt. They continue,

"America's Patton and Germany's Rommel, who as tacticians shone above all other army commanders."

The reason they wanted them silenced is because MacArthur and Patton understood the communist threat and were willing to speak out about it. Despite the fact that the politicians and the media attempted to vilify these two great men, General MacArthur and General Patton were not only great generals, they were great patriots.

General George S. Patton

George Smith Patton Jr. (November 11, 1885 – December 21, 1945) was a General of the United States Army who commanded the U.S. Seventh Army in the Mediterranean theater of World War II, and the U.S. Third Army in France and Germany following the Allied invasion of Normandy in June 1944. Patton attended the Virginia Military Institute and graduated from the U.S. Military Academy at West Point in 1909. Patton first saw combat during the Pancho Villa Expedition in 1916. The Pancho Villa Expedition was a military operation conducted by the United States Army against the paramilitary forces of Mexican revolutionary Francisco "Pancho" Villa during the Mexican Revolution of 1910–1920.

As part of the newly formed United States Tank Corps of the American Expeditionary Forces he saw action in World War I. Displaying courage that not even his bitterest enemies could deny, he led the charge against German machine guns. As he approached the German lines, he was badly wounded by a piece of shrapnel. Patton was awarded the Purple Heart and the Distinguished Service Medal for his service.

Patton led U.S. troops into the Mediterranean theater with an invasion of Casablanca during Operation Torch in 1942, and soon established himself as an effective commander through his rapid rehabilitation of the demoralized U.S. II Corps. He commanded the U.S. Seventh Army during the Allied invasion of Sicily, where he was the first Allied commander to reach Messina. Following the invasion of Normandy in June 1944, Patton was given command of the Third Army, which conducted a highly successful rapid armored drive across France. Under his decisive leadership, the Third Army took the lead in relieving beleaguered American troops at Bastogne during the Battle of the Bulge, after which his forces drove deep into Nazi Germany by the end of the war.

His strong emphasis on rapid and aggressive offensive action proved effective, and the concept of bold, highly mobile, armored operations became associated with his name. Everywhere Patton went, he won. The men who served under him loved him, while his enemies respected and feared him. After the war, many German generals claimed he was the best Allied general. They were right.[92]

There were what appeared to be multiple attempts on General Patton's life, and it was well known that he was feared and hated by the Nazis, the Soviets, American politicians, and people in the military. Patton wanted to go to the Far East and join MacArthur in the fight against the Japanese, but due to his outspoken dislike of the Soviets, he was banished to Bad Nauheim, Germany as Commanding Officer, 15th Army. Severely injured in an auto accident which, many believe was an assassination attempt, he died in Germany twelve days later, on December 21, 1945.

General Douglas MacArthur

Douglas MacArthur (January 26, 1880 – April 5, 1964) was an American five-star general and Field Marshal of the Philippine Army. He was Chief of Staff of the United States Army during the 1930s and played a prominent role in the Pacific theater during World War II. He received the Medal of Honor for his service in the Philippines Campaign.

Raised in a military family he was First Captain at the United States Military Academy at West Point, where he graduated top of the class of 1903. During the 1914 United States occupation of Veracruz, he conducted a reconnaissance mission, for which he was nominated for the Medal of Honor. In 1917, he was promoted from major to colonel and became chief of staff of the 42nd (Rainbow) Division. In the fighting on the Western Front during World War I, he rose to the rank of brigadier general, was again nominated for a Medal of Honor, and was awarded the Distinguished Service Cross twice and the Silver Star seven times.

From 1919 to 1922, MacArthur served as Superintendent of the U.S. Military Academy at West Point. In 1925, he became the Army's youngest major general. In 1930, he became Chief of Staff of the United States Army. MacArthur was recalled to active duty in 1941 as commander of United States Army Forces in the Far East. A series of disasters followed, starting with the destruction of his air forces on December 8, 1941, and the invasion of the Philippines by the Japanese. MacArthur's forces were soon compelled to withdraw to Bataan, where they held out until May 1942.

In March 1942, MacArthur, his family and his staff left nearby Corregidor Island in PT boats and escaped to Australia, where MacArthur became Supreme

Commander, Southwest Pacific Area. Upon his arrival, MacArthur gave a speech in which he famously promised "I shall return" to the Philippines. After more than two years of fighting in the Pacific, he fulfilled that promise. For his defense of the Philippines, MacArthur was awarded the Medal of Honor.

He officially accepted Japan's surrender on September 2, 1945, aboard the USS Missouri anchored in Tokyo Bay, and oversaw the occupation of Japan from 1945 to 1951. As the effective ruler of Japan, he oversaw sweeping economic, political and social changes, which put Japan on the path to become one of the world's most successful nations.

He led the United Nations Command in the Korean War. Despite heavy odds against him, he stopped the communist advance near the port of Pusan and with the Inchon landing. During the next two months the North Korean army was routed and all but destroyed.

Contrary to the failed strategy of Truman, MacArthur urged the bombing of communist bases in Manchuria, the blockade of the Chinese coast, and employment of Nationalist Chinese forces based on Formosa. General MacArthur was relieved of his command by President Truman on April 11, 1951, because Truman did not like the fact that MacArthur wanted to win the Korean War, not hand North Korea over to the communists.

The Balance of Power at the end of World War II

The Soviet Union was facing extinction as German forces closed in on Moscow, laid siege to Leningrad, and seized Kiev. Without the increased pressure to defend the German homeland from British and American forces, and substantial aid from the US Lend-Lease program, the Soviet Union would have fallen in total defeat. The Soviet Union lost approximately 27,000,000 people during the war.

The USSR was technologically well behind Great Britain and the United States. Stalin was aware of the backwardness of the Soviet military, industry and manufacturing, and technology relative to the West, and the 1946-50 five-year plan included a special focus on developing (stealing) four new technologies including atomic weapons, rockets, jet engines, and radar. Stalin's regime got a head start on these developments, when the US allowed the Soviets to capture a substantial portion of Nazi Germany's aircraft production facilities and reaping the scientific and engineering benefits of German research. In addition, the USSR seized three US B-29s that had been forced down in the Soviet Far East and reverse engineered them to produce the Tu-4 bomber in

1947. The British were complicit in assisting the Soviets in their quest to gain technological and military parity with the West when they allowed the Soviets to purchase advanced Rolls-Royce Nene and Derwent centrifugal-flow engines to increase the performance of the swept-winged fighter that the MiG design team began producing in 1948.[93]

The Soviet Union had no significant atomic bomb program during World War II and its long-range bomber force was almost non-existent. After the American bombing of Hiroshima and Nagasaki in 1945, Stalin ordered a crash program in a desperate attempt to catch up with the US. The prospecting, mining, and chemical processing of the uranium and plutonium for the early bombs was an enormous industrial undertaking that cost nearly 2 percent of Soviet GNP and required the labor of hundreds of thousands of workers, many of them from the Gulag labor camps.

Stalin insisted that the first Soviet bomb follow the stolen American design and the resulting RDS-1 fission bomb was successfully detonated on August 29, 1949. It was followed by the detonation of an indigenous Soviet design, the RDS-2, on September 24, 1951.

Besides shortcomings in nuclear weapons delivery, shortages in fissionable material meant that series production of Soviet nuclear weapons did not begin until 1953-54. As a result, the Soviet Union had very little capability to conduct intercontinental nuclear strikes through the end of Stalin's reign in 1953.[94]

At the end of World War II, the Soviet Navy was essentially non-existent. In both the Baltic and Black Seas, the Kremlin did not have a naval component, whereas Great Britain and the United States were well established sea powers. As is typical of the Soviets and communists in general, what they cannot develop they steal. The Soviets learned quickly, especially from captured German experts and warships, including German U-boats that were to be incorporated into the Soviet Navy. Using the German method of submarine construction, building submarines in sections and then welding them together, the Soviets managed to increase their production. In 1950, the Soviets used this technique to good effect in their Whisky class modeled after the German Type XXI design. The Kremlin found it impossible to build aircraft carriers owing to the fragile state of the Soviet economy. Instead, the Soviet Navy relied on shore-based aviation.[95]

The USSR did not have the economic or military resources to defend its massive Pacific coastline, let alone challenge US naval superiority in the region. By the end of the war, Soviet GDP was $383 billion, compared to a GDP of $1.498 trillion for the United States.[96]

The Allied Powers could have destroyed the Russian communists but failed to do so. After the second Great War, the Russians were in a weakened state. They had limited weapons and outdated technology. Their economy had been destroyed. The Americans and their allies could have easily defeated them. General Patton, Commanding General of the American 3rd Armored Division was quite correct when he said, "We promised the Europeans freedom. It would be worse than dishonorable not to see they have it. This might mean war with the Russians, but what of it? They have no Air Force anymore; their gasoline and ammunition supplies are low. I've seen their miserable supply trains; mostly wagons draw by beaten up old horses or oxen. I'll say this; the Third Army alone with very little help and with damned few casualties, could lick what is left of the Russians in six weeks."

Betrayal and Capitulation

When looking at the betrayal and capitulation to Stalin by Roosevelt, one has to look no further than the communist takeover of the United States government by the Soviets. For most people, this is inconceivable and beyond belief, but it is indeed a true sad fact. The treasonous acts by Roosevelt and his administration were only exposed later and the people responsible were never punished. Unfortunately, the consequences of their heinous actions are still being felt today.

The extent of the communist infiltration of the Roosevelt administration is staggering. Chief Special Agent Guy Hottel summed up the matter in a March 1946 memo to FBI Director Hoover:

It has become increasingly clear in the investigation of this case that there are a tremendous number of persons employed in the United States government who are communists and strive daily to advance the cause of communism and destroy the foundations of this government... Today nearly every department or agency of this government is infiltrated with them in varying degree. To aggravate the situation, they appear to have concentrated most heavily in those departments which make policy, particularly in the international field, or carry it into effect... such organizations as the State and Treasury departments, Federal Economic Administration (FEA), Office of Strategic Service (OSS), War Production Board (WPB), etc. Apart from Russian espionage inherent in this case, there has emerged already the picture of a large, energetic and capable number of communists, including suspects who operate daily in the legislative field, as well as in the executive branch of government.[97]

The extent of the infiltration of American (or naturalized) communists into the federal government was no fantasy of emotional persons. This record will show that the names of these persons, pledged to the principles and methods enunciated from Moscow and to serving the purposes of the Soviet government, had gained strategic positions in the White House, in the Armed Services, in every government department, and even on the staffs of some Congressional committees. They were sent on foreign missions to Russia, Germany, France, Italy, Britain, Latin America, China, and elsewhere. They became secretaries and advisors at important international conferences.[98]

As President Hoover points out: "Moscow undertook four great conspiracies against the American people, the first being the activities of our [American] Communist Party in organizing public opinion; the second, their control of certain great labor unions; the third, their capture of otherwise harmless activities, such as the Institute of Pacific Relations; the fourth, and worst, being infiltration of their members and fellow travelers into high policy-making positions in Roosevelt's administration, and fifth, infiltration into education." [99]

Perhaps the most damaging infiltration of the United States was the infiltration of the international affairs departments such as the intelligence services and the State Department. Among the many communists in the Roosevelt administration was the Ambassador to Moscow, Joseph Davies. Davies was shameless in his adulation of Stalin and refused to report the devastating famine and horrible atrocities occurring in the Soviet Union in the 1930's. Similarly, the communist propaganda newspaper, *The New York Times*, Pulitzer Prize winning Moscow correspondent, Walter Duranty, another Stalin lover, but one with tremendous influence, continually omitted the Soviet Unions' failed and devastating economic policies, and Stalin's brutal purges and gulags from his reporting about Russia. [100]

Harry Hopkins on a trip home from Yalta stated that Roosevelt: "had frequently spoken of the respect and admiration he had for Marshal Stalin and was looking forward to their next meeting." Harry Hopkins was a social worker married to a radical feminist, and a key architect of the socialist New Deal including the Works Progress Administration (WPA). The WPA was a New Deal program that was used to buy votes and create propaganda to further Roosevelt's socialist agenda.

Whether Harry Hopkins was officially a Soviet agent or not is debatable. What is not debatable is the fact that he admired Stalin, and he was a pro-Soviet communist who put Soviet interests above those of the United States. Harry Hopkins lived in the White House with President Roosevelt for three years.

Roosevelt frowned on spying on the Russians and was committed to showing good intentions to the Soviet Union. He was so concerned he might upset 'Uncle Joe'

Stalin that he ordered General William Donovan of the Office of Strategic Service (OSS) to inform the Soviets of the existence of the OSS and its activities. The Office of Strategic Services (OSS) was a wartime intelligence agency of the United States during World War II, and a predecessor of the modern Central Intelligence Agency (CIA). General Donovan outlined the organization aims, scope of operations, etc., giving details of specific types of operations, means of communication, and organizations of groups within enemy countries.[101]

Although it was treason to provide information to the Soviets about the OSS and its operations, it didn't really matter. There were so many communists in the US government that by the time Donovan outlined the operations of the OSS, the Soviets had already infiltrated the organization.

The Counter Intelligence Corps (CIC) was a World War II and early Cold War intelligence agency within the United States Army. Within the United States the CIC, in collaboration with the Provost Marshal General and the Federal Bureau of Investigation (FBI), carried out background checks on military personnel having access to classified material, investigations of possible sabotage and subversion, and allegations of disloyalty. Roosevelt ordered in 1943, that the Counter Intelligence Corps (CIC) "cease any investigations of known or suspected communists and destroy all files on such persons immediately." [102]

By the 1940's, the FBI had already grasped the problem of communist infiltration of the US government. Roosevelt, Truman and Eisenhower all ignored the warnings of McCarthy and the FBI. Whether Truman was a communist is debatable. His capitulation to the communists in the Korean War is certainly questionable. He could have just been clueless or ill-informed and there is some evidence that he was not informed of all the subversive activities of the infiltrators. There were some who tried to educate Truman, as can be seen from General Wedemeyer's report to President Truman and Secretary of State Marshall on September 19, 1947:

… "The goals and the lofty aims of freedom-loving peoples are jeopardized…by [communist] forces as sinister as those that operated in Europe and Asia during the ten years leading to World War II. The pattern is familiar – employment of subversive agents; infiltration tactics; incitement of disorder and chaos to disrupt normal economy and thereby to undermine popular confidence in government and leaders; seizure of authority without reference to the will of the people – all the techniques skillfully designed and ruthlessly implemented in order to create favorable conditions for the imposition of totalitarian ideologies…" [103]

What the FBI found was vast infiltration of every branch of the US government. As pointed out by Robert K. Wilcox in *Target Patton*, 'Senator McCarthy, whatever his personal faults, has been wrongly portrayed by a largely biased left-wing press and Hollywood whose distortions have left an impression on ordinary Americans that McCarthy was a bullying, lying, demigod. The truth is, he was correct and a patriot in his accusations that the immediate post-war Truman government was rife with communists.'

But what do they teach children at our public schools? From the AP US History we get the following lie: "McCarthy failed to uncover a single communist. His practice of making unsubstantiated accusations of disloyalty without evidence became known as

McCarthyism." There were hundreds of identified communists in the United States government. For lists and details of the communist infiltrators see Herbert Hoover's *Freedom Betrayed,* M. Stanton Evans *Blacklisted by History: The Untold Story of Senator Joe McCarthy,* and Diana West's *American Betrayal.*

Generations of young minds have been and continue to be brainwashed with left wing propaganda and lies. The same communists of the anti-McCarthy era are engaged in communist lies and propaganda today. These include all the major broadcast and cable networks NBC, ABC, CBS, CNN, media outlets including *Time-Life*, the *New York Times*, the *LA Times*, the *Washington Post*, local and regional newspapers, and a slew of left-wing journalists from most major media outlets on the Internet and across the country. Incredibly, the United States government, using your tax dollars, continues to support organizations such as the National Endowment for the Arts (NEA) and the Public Broadcasting System (PBS) that are nothing more than propaganda outlets for the radical left.

The Atomic Bomb

There were numerous acts of treason committed before, during and after World War II, but by far the greatest act of treason was to assist the Soviet Union in the development of nuclear weapons. This was truly the greatest act of treason in the history of the world. Without a restraining mechanism, it wasn't long before the rest of the world would acquire nuclear weapons.

The Manhattan Project was the American program for researching and developing the first atomic bomb. The weapons produced were based solely upon the principles of nuclear fission of uranium 235 and plutonium 239, chain reactions liberating immense amounts of destructive heat energy. Although originally established in Manhattan, New York by the Manhattan Engineer District of the U.S. Army Corps of Engineers, the majority of the research took place under director General Leslie Groves at the Los Alamos laboratory in New Mexico. The scientific director was the known communist Robert Oppenheimer. Incredibly, General Groves knew that Robert Oppenheimer was a communist but still named him as scientific director.

The pattern of communists in the US government continues today. President Obama, a Marxist himself, put a known communist, John Brennan, in charge of the United States Central Intelligence Agency.[104] Brennan has even admitted that he voted for a Communist Party candidate. He doesn't appear to care if people are communists or drug addicts either. Stating, "We've all had indiscretions in our past," adding neither drug experimentation nor activism should stop people from being put in charge of the most sensitive positions in the government.

Soviet intelligence first learned of Anglo-American talk of an atomic bomb program in September 1941, almost a year before the Manhattan Engineer District (MED) was created. The information likely came from John Cairncross, a member of the infamous "Cambridge Five" spies in Britain. Cairncross served as a private secretary for a British government official, Lord Hankey, who was privy to some British discussions of the MAUD Report. Another of the "Cambridge Five," Donald Maclean, also sent word of the potential for an atomic bomb to his Soviet handlers around the same time. Maclean was a key Soviet agent. In 1947 and 1948, he served as a British liaison with the MED's successor, the Atomic Energy Commission.

The MAUD committee was created to perform the research required to determine if applying nuclear technology to make a bomb was, in reality, feasible. The result of the committee's work was the MAUD report, which reviewed the feasibility and necessity of an atomic bomb for the war effort. In response to the report's findings, the British created a nuclear weapons project officially named Tube Alloys. The MAUD report was made available to the United States, where it energized the American effort, which became the Manhattan Project.

Due to the large size of the pre-existing Soviet espionage network within the United States, and the number of Americans who were sympathetic to communism or members of the Communist Party of the United States of America (CPUSA), few aspects of the Manhattan Project remained secret from the Soviet Union.

The Soviet Union proved more adept at espionage than America or Britain, primarily because it was able to play on the ideological sympathies of a significant number of Americans and British as well as foreign émigrés. Soviet intelligence services devoted a tremendous amount of resources into spying on the United States and Britain. In the United States alone, hundreds of Americans provided secret information to the Soviet Union, and the quality of Soviet sources in Britain was even better. In contrast, due to President Roosevelt's appeasement of Stalin during the war, neither the American nor the British secret services had a single agent in Moscow. The CPUSA had thousands of members, a disproportionate number of whom were highly educated and likely to work in high level government positions and sensitive wartime industries. Many physicists were members of the CPUSA before the war.

The Manhattan Project never had an official charter establishing it and defining its mission, but two documents in 1942 from Vannevar Bush to President Roosevelt are the functional equivalent of a charter, in terms of presidential approvals for the mission, not to mention for a huge budget. In a progress report, Vannevar Bush, Director, Office of Scientific Research and Development, told President Roosevelt that the bomb project was on a pilot plant basis, but not yet at the production stage.[105]

Some months later, with the Manhattan Project already underway and under the direction of General Leslie Grove, Bush outlined to Roosevelt the effort necessary to produce six fission bombs with the goal of having enough fissile material by the first half of 1945 to produce the bombs.

While the American atomic bomb project was successfully completing its mission, the Soviet program was plagued by an array of problems. The Soviet scientists were not as technologically advanced as their success might have indicated, as they had never before obtained uranium and needed the aid of German scientist Nikolaus Riehl to develop uranium suitable for a reactor. Vasily S. Yemelyanov, a Soviet scientist working on the project, explained in 1987 that the Soviets were not even sure that their plutonium was plutonium.[106]

The Soviets also had limited resources of uranium and graphite, lacked Geiger counters, used impure uranium that lacked the proper number of neutrons for a chain reaction, and employed a very poor diffusion technique, using a metal sheet with pin punched holes as the barrier for gaseous diffusion. German refugee scientists were needed to develop nickel pipes gauged to the proper porosity for diffusion.[107]

Progress was further limited by the fact that the Soviets could not develop reactor grade uranium or plutonium and attacked the problem with simplistic engineering procedures, and an inadequate mathematics team. Although they had competent theoretical scientists, the Soviets had a long history of problems with the practical application of physics.

The Soviets knew they didn't have the technical capabilities required to build a bomb so they rounded up captured German scientists to join their program. Riehl estimates that without the aid of German scientists, the bomb project would have taken an additional 1-2 years.[108]

Between the years 1942 and 1954, the KGB obtained thousands of pages of technical information about the Manhattan Project. Sergei Leskov reports that this information included: calculations for the construction of the plutonium charge; calculations for the critical mass of fissile material; information on detonation devices; information on the gaseous diffusion factory that produced U-235; information about a plutonium production report; a report on the study of secondary neutrons; a report on the metallurgy of uranium and plutonium; and information on the kinetics of atomic reactions.[109]

Kurchatov admitted in a memo of March 4, 1943, that certain information "came as a surprise to our physicists and chemists," such as the centrifugal method of isotope separation. The Soviets also had reached an impasse on the "problem of nuclear explosion and combustion." Stolen documents revealed that this problem could be rectified by mixing uranium oxide and heavy water together - a method the Soviet scientists' thought was impossible. [110]

Furthermore, Klaus Fuchs, a German scientist who worked on the Manhattan and British Tube Alloy

Projects, and who was one of the primary Soviet atom bomb spies, confessed to the U.S. War Department and FBI on January 27, 1950, that he had given the Soviet Union the principle design of the plutonium bomb.[111] In his confession of January 30, 1950, he admitted that the information about the plutonium bomb included material on the use of implosion detonation rather than the gun technique, the critical mass for plutonium bombs (5-15 kilograms), information on the solid plutonium core, details of the initiator, specifying that it used 50 curies of polonium, the two types of explosives, "Baratol" and "Composition B," and "full details of the tamper, aluminum shell, and high explosive lens system." He also provided the equations of state of the bomb, information about the problems of pre-detonation, the blast calculations for Hiroshima and Nagasaki, and the ideal ignition temperature. All told, Fuchs provided the Soviets with "the size of the bomb, what it contained, how it was constructed, and how it was detonated." [112]

There were many other conspirators including, Allan Nunn May, who gave samples of enriched U-235 to his Soviet contact for analysis.[113] David Greenglass also provided the Soviets with a drawing of the implosion lens, and Igor Gouzenko reported the exact amount of U-235 used daily at the U.S. metallurgical laboratory.[114]

The espionage information was so complete and valuable to the Soviets that when the USSR began to build its atomic installation, "its plutonium plant was almost identical in size and specifications to 'secret' Reactor 305 at Hanford, Washington."

A July 10, 1945 letter from NKGB director V. N. Merkulov to Beria is an example of how much information the Soviets had on the Manhattan Project. Merkulov reported that the United States had scheduled the test of a nuclear device for that same day, although the actual test took place 6 days later. According to Merkulov, two fissile materials were being produced: element-49 (plutonium), and U-235; the test device was fueled by plutonium. The Soviet source reported that the weight of the device was 3 tons (which was in the ball park) and forecast an explosive yield of 5 kilotons. That figure was based on underestimates by Manhattan Project scientists: the actual yield of the test device was 20 kilotons.

Not only did the US provide the technical information for building the atomic bomb to the Soviets, they provided them with the materials to build it. Lend Lease expeditor Major George Jordan stated, "I became aware that certain folders were being held to one side on Colonel Kotikov's desk for the accumulation of a very special chemical plant. In fact, this chemical plant was referred to by Colonel Kotikov as a "bomb powder" factory. By referring to my diary, and checking the items I now know went into an atomic energy plant, I am able to show the following records starting with the year 1942, while I was still at Newark. These materials, which are necessary for the creation of atomic pile, moved to Russia in 1942: Graphite: natural, flake, lump or chip, costing American taxpayers $812,437, Over thirteen million dollars' worth of aluminum tubes (used in the atomic pile to "cook" or transmute the uranium into plutonium), the exact amount being $13,041,152. We sent 834,989 pounds of cadmium metal for rods to control the intensity of an atomic pile; the cost was $781,472, the really secret material, thorium, finally showed up and started going through immediately. The amount during 1942 was 13,440 pounds at a cost of $22,848. On Jan. 30, 1943 we shipped an additional 11,912 pounds of thorium nitrate to Russia from Philadelphia on the S.S. John C. Fremont." [115]

General Leslie Groves would later testify before Congress in 1949, that his operation came under continuous pressure to release experimental atomic materials to the USSR from the Lend-Lease office. "We didn't want this material shipped, yet they [officials from Lend-Lease] kept coming back and coming back." [116]

Further testimony by FBI Agent Donald Appell stated: "As to the shipment of uranium and heavy water, two specific shipments of uranium oxide and nitrate and shipments of heavy water have been completely documented to include even the number of the plane that flew the uranium and heavy water out of Great Falls." [117]

With the assistance of German scientists and the Roosevelt administration, and the breakneck pace demanded by Beria, the project was finished by mid-August 1949. Lavrentiy Beria was a Soviet politician of Georgian ethnicity, Marshal of the Soviet Union and state security administrator, and chief of the Soviet security and secret police apparatus (NKVD) under Joseph Stalin during World War II.

On August 29, 1949, five years after the American bombing of Hiroshima and Nagasaki, the Soviet Union detonated an atomic plutonium bomb. The device they used was virtually identical in design to the one that had been tested at Trinity four years previously. [118]

The Roosevelt administration, and most likely Roosevelt himself, knew that materials and technical information related to the Manhattan Project and the atomic bomb was being provided to the Soviets. They knew and they even expedited the transfers. All one has to do is look at the scale of the Soviet sympathizers and apologists in the Roosevelt administration and it is easy to see why the US monopoly on nuclear weapons would not last long.

After World War II the United States was the only country that possessed nuclear weapons, which if necessary, would have allowed them to easily destroy the Russian and Chinese communists. The Western powers failure to end communism when they had the chance, led directly to the deaths of over 100 million humans.

The United States and their allies have a history of appeasement and capitulation. Not only did they hand over Eastern Europe and North Korea to the Russian and Chinese communists, the United States had the opportunity to halt the spread of nuclear weapons. They could have built a peaceful and just world devoid of nuclear weapons but lacked the foresight and backbone. There are now nine countries, including the two rogue nations of Pakistan and North Korea, which together possess more than 15,000 nuclear weapons. The leaders of the time knew the dangers of the irrational belief system of communism, nonetheless they believed in the impossible utopian ideals of the communist faith. This flawed faith, allowed the communists to rise to power in China and Russia. The Western powers failure to terminate communism is why there are three global powers rather than one.

Until the Soviets produced an atomic weapon and began to deploy it as an offensive weapon they were, according to the American left, our friends and allies, champions of the new socialist world order. Although too late, the world finally realized what the Soviets were after all along; world domination.

What Could Have Been

Today, as in the past, ideology and power politics rule rather than reason and a desire to do what is right based on reason, facts, and evidence. The human race might not be united, but without socialism, communism, and the spread of nuclear weapons, there is no question that the world would be a far better place. The United States could have defeated two evil regimes, Germany and the Soviet Union. Instead, it strengthened the Soviets, one of the most evil, brutal regimes in history and helped create the equally evil regime of Mao and the totalitarian state of China.

While people may disagree on historical interpretations and processes, no one but a communist can disagree with the indefensible results:

1. President Roosevelt and his administration saved the evil Stalin and the Soviet communists from certain destruction.
2. President Roosevelt and his administration handed Eastern Europe to the Soviet Union.
3. President Roosevelt and his administration put Mao and the communists into power in China.

4. President Roosevelt and his administration gave the atomic bomb to the Soviet Union.

As a direct result of the actions of Roosevelt and his communist conspirators, the United States saved the evilest empire ever created in human history, then gave them the most powerful weapon ever developed by humans. There is no greater crime against humanity then what Roosevelt and his fellow communists did to the world.

Away from the fog of power politics and war, and as the true intentions of the communists sunk in, many leaders realized what they had done. By supporting Stalin and the communists, they supported an evil far worse than the Nazis.

No one could be stupid enough to believe that Stalin was a good man. This can only mean that Roosevelt was delusional, or that he was a communist. Truman was no better. After meeting Josef Stalin at the Potsdam conference in July 1945, President Harry S. Truman wrote in his diary: "I can deal with Stalin. He is honest- but smart as hell."

Churchill was one of the few who understood the Soviet threat. Unfortunately, he was powerless against Stalin and Roosevelt. "Churchill was the only man in a position of power who knew what we were walking into," Patton said. "He wanted to get into the Balkans and Central Europe to keep the Russians at bay. He wanted to get into Berlin and Prague and get to the Baltic coast on the North. Churchill had a sense of history. Unfortunately, some of our leaders were just damn fools who had no idea of Russian history. Hell, I doubt if they even knew Russia, just less than 100 years ago, owned Finland, sucked the blood out of Poland, and were using Siberia as a prison for their own people. How Stalin must have sneered when he got through with them at all those phony conferences." [119]

Privately, Churchill suggested that America strike first, before it was too late. According to FBI records, he urged Sen. Styles Bridges, a conservative Republican from New Hampshire active in foreign affairs, to back a preemptory and devastating attack on Moscow. "He [Churchill] pointed out that if an atomic bomb could be dropped on the Kremlin wiping it out, it would be a very easy problem to handle the balance of Russia, which would be without direction," Bridges told the FBI.

During a "private conference with Churchill" while visiting Europe in the summer of 1947, Bridges claimed the former prime minister had "stated that the only salvation for the civilization of the world would be if the President of the United States would declare Russia to be imperiling world peace and attack Russia." If this wasn't done, according to the FBI report dated December 5, 1947, Churchill predicted "Russia will attack the United States in the next two or three years when she gets the atomic bomb and civilization will be wiped out or set back many years." A full-fledged nuclear attack on the Kremlin didn't seem to faze Bridges, who'd been a sharp policy critic of Roosevelt and Truman.

If the United States would have not have been taken over by the communists, 100 million people who died as a result of communism would be alive today. Every socialist experiment that has been attempted has been a total failure. New Harmony, the kibbutz, the Soviet Union, all failures. The socialist experiments that have destroyed so many countries and lives would have never occurred. Countries such as Russia, China, North Korea, Cambodia, Chile, Argentina, Cuba, Ethiopia, (other African countries) and Venezuela.

There are many modern iterations of communism using different names to deceive the masses. These include liberals, globalists, progressives, and socialists, but they are all just communists. Communism is nothing more than a cruel hoax perpetuated on the gullible masses; a hoax being a deception, or to deceive by a story or trick for mischief. With hypocrisy and lies, the communists attempt to manipulate the masses with talk of support and salvation for the poor, inequality, oppression and social justice. Promising people something they know they cannot deliver. Any attempt to socially engineer a communist utopia will only lead to greater misery for the masses.

Communism, socialism, fascism, progressivism, egalitarianism; you can call it what you want, but it is all the same thing, tyranny. Unlike communism, capitalism is not based on faith, it is a rational economic system based on free markets which are the natural mechanism of human interaction. You cannot reprogram human nature. There are always some humans that will want to possess more than another, and there will always be free riders who wish to reap all the benefits but contribute none of the work.

The socialists and communists consider themselves intellectuals, but there is nothing intellectual in believing in faith over reason, or in denying facts and evidence. Studying nonsensical dogma does not make one an intellectual. If these true believers were in fact intellectuals, they would dismiss Marxism-Leninism for what it is, garbage. If you are a communist not only are you stupid, you are a supporter of evil and the enslavement of the human species.

After looking at all the facts you can only come to one conclusion. The US government under Roosevelt supported the Soviet Union because they believed in the goal of a world socialist revolution. The decades of suffering and misery in Eastern Europe under Soviet rule were a direct result of Roosevelt's pact with Stalin. Roosevelt told Averell Harriman, that "he didn't care whether the countries bordering Russian become communized." The disgraceful leaders sat back and watched as Stalin and Russia enslaved half of Europe. This was done after the Americans and their allies sacrificed millions of their fighting men to liberate these same countries from the Germans. No one with any moral fiber, who believes in liberty and democracy, would have allowed the communists to enslave Eastern Europe.

The consequences of losing the war against communism are staggering. The misery and suffering that were a direct result of this defeat are a disgrace to the human race. It is obvious that had the Soviet Union been defeated by the Germans many of the wars after WWII would not have occurred. As direct result of the United States' failure to stop communism when they had the chance, there were multiple events that led to the death of millions of people. These events include Mao's Red Terror in China, the Korean War, the Vietnam War, and the Cambodian genocide.

As a direct result of the failed policies and Chinese Communist support by the Roosevelt and Truman administrations, an estimated 65 million Chinese died as a result of Mao's Red Terror; the repeated, merciless attempts to create a new socialist China. In order to accomplish his socialist transformation, Mao implemented the Great Leap Forward and the Cultural Revolution.

The Great Leap Forward was an economic and social campaign by the Communist Party of China (CPC) from 1958 to 1962. The campaign's goal was to rapidly transform the country from an agrarian economy into a socialist society through rapid industrialization and collectivization. The Great Leap Forward included the introduction of mandatory agricultural collectivization. Private farming was prohibited, and those engaged in it were labeled counter-revolutionaries.

The Great Leap Forward was an incredible failure. At least 45 million people died from the resulting famine and persecution from 1958 to 1962.[120] Not all deaths during the Great Leap were from starvation. An estimated 2.5 million people were beaten or tortured to death, and one million to three million committed suicide.[121]

The Cultural Revolution was a sociopolitical movement in China from 1966 to 1976. Its stated goal was to preserve Chinese Communism by purging remnants of capitalist and traditional elements from Chinese society, and to re-impose Maoism as the dominant ideology within the Communist Party by purging intellectuals and party officials considered to be counter-revolutionaries.

The number of people that died as a result of the Cultural Revolution varies and the true number may never be known. In *Mao: The Unknown Story*, Jung Chang and Jon Halliday claim that as many as 3 million people died in the violence of the Cultural Revolution.[122] The Holocaust memorial museum puts the death toll between 5 and 10 million.[123]

In 1951, Judge Irving Kaufman, in sentencing the Rosenberg's to death stated, the accelerated acquisition of nuclear weapons by the Soviets "caused the communist aggression in Korea, with the resultant casualties exceeding 50,000, and who knows but that millions more of innocent people may pay the price of your treason." There is no doubt that Stalin was emboldened to start the war in Korea once he had possession of nuclear weapons.

According to the data from the U.S. Department of Defense, the United States suffered 33,686 battle deaths, along with 2,830 non-battle deaths, during the Korean War. South Korea reported some 373,599 civilian and 137,899 military deaths. Western sources estimate the Chinese Peoples Volunteer Army (PVA) suffered about 400,000 killed and 486,000 wounded, while the Korean People's Army (KPA) suffered 215,000 killed and 303,000 wounded.

Data from official Chinese sources, on the other hand, reported that the Chinese PVA had suffered 114,000 battle deaths, 34,000 non-battle deaths, 340,000 wounded, 7,600 missing and during the war. 7,110 Chinese POWs were repatriated to China. Chinese sources also reported that North Korea had suffered 290,000 casualties, 90,000 captured and a large number of civilian deaths. The Encyclopedia Britannica stated that North Korean civilian casualties were 600,000, while South Korean civilian casualties reached one million. Recent scholarship puts the full battle death toll on all sides at just over 1.2 million.

The Cambodian genocide was carried out by the regime of the Khmer Rouge (KR) on any individual that was perceived to be in opposition. The regime was led by Pol Pot, who controlled the government from 1975 to 1979, killing approximately 1.5 to 3 million Cambodians.

The regime wanted to start a new republic and turn the country into a socialist agrarian republic, founded on the policies of Marxism-Leninism and Maoism. During his second year of rule in 1976, the Khmer Rouge changed the name of the country and established Democratic Kampuchea, symbolizing the start of a new republic. In order to fulfill the regime's goals, they emptied the cities and forced Cambodians to be relocated into labor camps in the countryside, where they were tortured and where mass executions, use of forced labor, physical abuse, malnutrition and disease were prevalent. This led to the death of approximately 25 percent of Cambodia's total population.

Anyone perceived as the opposition was taken to the Killing Fields, located outside the capital city Phnom Penh where they were executed (mainly by pickaxes to save bullets) and buried in mass graves. The Vietnamese invasion of Cambodia ended the genocide and the Khmer Rouge regime in 1979.

Another war that was a direct result of the Stalin-Roosevelt pact was the Vietnam War. More than 58,000 United States troops died and another 300,000 were wounded. The war killed an estimated 2 million Vietnamese civilians, 1.1 million North Vietnamese troops, and over 200,000 South Vietnamese soldiers. None of these atrocities would have occurred if someone would have had the backbone to stand up to Roosevelt and the communists.

G. J. Meyer's observation on World War I applies to war in general. In his book *A World Undone, The Story of the Great War 1914 to 1918*, he writes:

> Anyone inclined to believe that some dark force beyond human comprehension intervened again and again to make the Great War long and ruinous would have no difficulty in finding evidence to support such a thesis. There is no better example than the Battle of Verdun, which in its length and cost and brutality and finally in its sheer pointlessness has always and rightly been seen as a perfect microcosm of the war itself.

In the aftermath of World War II, the costs and brutality, the pointlessness, the millions sacrificed, are all on terrible display. The defeat of one tyrant merely led to the salvation of another.

The damage done by Roosevelt was not restricted to his treasonous acts during and after World War II. He also put the United States on the downward path towards socialism. The government caused the great depression, then made it worse, and then prolonged it by their foolish attempts to manage the economy. Like all socialists, they believed they could manage the economy better than free markets. By implementing price and wage controls, they distorted markets, and created imbalances and misallocation of resources in the economy. Central to the economic system of capitalism is the idea that markets set a price for goods and services that matches the supply and demand. Scarcity, choice, utility, and cost are the ideas that underlie supply and demand. In a market system, scarce goods are rationed by prices. Employment and prosperity would have returned much faster without the destructive and foolish intervention by the Hoover and Roosevelt administrations.

During the first year of President Roosevelt's New Deal, he called for increasing federal spending to $10 billion while revenues were only $3 billion. Between 1933 and 1936, government expenditures rose by more than 83 percent. Federal debt skyrocketed by 73 percent. Roosevelt signed off on legislation that raised the top income tax rate to 79 percent and then later to 90 percent. In addition, Roosevelt accelerated the centralization and enlargement of the federal government. The government bureaucracy increased from 600,000 employees in 1932 to 2.4 million one year after the war.

Roosevelt had more plans for the economy, namely the National Labor Relations Act, better known as the "Wagner Act." This was a payoff to labor unions, and with these new powers, labor unions went on a militant organizing frenzy that included threats, boycotts, strikes, seizures of plants, widespread violence and other acts that pushed productivity down sharply and unemployment up dramatically. In 1938, Roosevelt's New Deal produced the nation's first depression within a depression. The stock market crashed again, losing nearly 50 percent of its value between August 1937 and March 1938, and unemployment climbed back to 20 percent.[124]

There are some who believe Roosevelt was more of a fascist then a socialist. Roosevelt himself called Mussolini "admirable" and professed that he was "deeply impressed by what he has accomplished." The admiration was mutual. In a laudatory review of Roosevelt's 1933 book *Looking Forward*, Mussolini wrote, "Reminiscent of Fascism is the principle that the state no longer leaves the economy to its own devices.... Without question, the mood accompanying this sea change resembles that of Fascism." The chief Nazi newspaper, Volkischer Beobachter, repeatedly praised "Roosevelt's adoption of National Socialist strains of thought in his economic and social policies" and "the development toward an authoritarian state" based on the "demand that collective good be put before individual self-interest."

It is also true that New Dealers openly collaborated with American Stalinists as part of the "Popular Front" during World War II. The Communist Party USA did not run a presidential candidate in 1944, choosing instead to endorse FDR for reelection.[125]

The Roosevelt communists were on their way to totally taking total control of the government, but there was one last obstacle, the Supreme Court; the one institution that, at the time, had not been taken over by the communists. The Supreme Court struck down the National Industrial Recovery Act (NIRA) and invalidated the Agricultural Adjustment Act (AAA).

Determined to implement his socialist economic plan, and prevent the Supreme Court from overturning or invalidating additional parts of the New Deal, Roosevelt requested authority to appoint new Supreme Court justices for every member older than 70 years old. This would have allowed Roosevelt to appoint six new justices and the communist coup would have been complete. Roosevelt's request was denied, but unfortunately, he managed to rig the court when several justices retired and Roosevelt appointed nine new members to the court. Even today, we are living with the consequences of the communist takeover of the Supreme Court.

Roosevelt's roommate, the communist Harry Hopkins, sounds no different from the politicians of today, "When a democratic victory is won, then the great wealth of the world must be shared with all people." He continues, "The days of the policy of 'the white man's burden' are over. Vast masses of people simply are not going to tolerate it and for the life of me I can't see why they should. We have left little in our trail except misery and poverty for the people we have exploited."

The sad fact is that the communists were never defeated, they are still here. They are in the government, in the unions, and have essentially taken control of public schools and universities. They continue to push their utopian worldview and will do anything to gain and keep power. The masses have been brainwashed by the media, left wing politicians, and the public schools and universities into believing that capitalism is an evil system of oppression, and that true American heroes, including Patton, MacArthur, McCarthy and others were the bad guys.

The global socialist movement began in Russia, spread to China, was accelerated under the Roosevelt administration, implemented in Europe, and has now infected most of the world. With the communist takeover of global media, education, and political institutions, the future of the world looks bleak. General MacArthur understood what was happening and was vilified by the left-wing politicians and media. What follows is his description of this sordid state of affairs.

But now strange voices are heard across the land, decrying this old and proven concept of patriotism. Seductive murmurs are arising that it is now outmoded by some more comprehensive and all-embracing philosophy, that we are provincial and immature or reactionary and stupid when we idealize our own country; that it is higher destiny for us under another and more general flag; that no longer when we send our sons and daughters to the battlefields must we see them through all the way to victory; that we can call upon them to fight and even to die in some halfhearted and indecisive way; that we can plunge them recklessly into war and then suddenly decide that it is a wrong war or in the wrong place or at a wrong time, or even that we can call it not a war at all by using some more euphemistic and gentler name; that we can treat them as expendable although they are our own flesh and blood; that we, the strongest military nation in the world, have suddenly become dependent upon others for our security and even our welfare. Listen not to these voices, be they from the one political party or the other. Be they from the high and mighty or the lowly and forgotten. Heed them not. Visit upon them a righteous scorn, born of the past sacrifices of your fighting sons and daughters. Repudiate them in the market place, on platforms, from the pulpit. The highest encomium you can still receive is to be called a patriot, if it means you love your country above all else and will place your life, if need be, at the service of your flag.[126]

Sadly, nationalism and its main component, patriotism, is now considered evil. The communists know that sovereign nations and patriotism stand in their way. As we see this dark fate enveloping the world, we should remember what General MacArthur and General Patton believed in more than anything else; duty, honor, country.

Sources and Notes

Socialism and Communism

1. *The Economist*, May 5, 2018, 79
2. Dr. Fred Schwarz, *You can Trust the Communists to be Communists,* (California, 1960), 7, 10

The Truth about Lenin

3. Dr. Fred Schwarz, *You can Trust the Communists to be Communists,* (California, 1960), 37
4. Victor Sebestyen, *Lenin, the Man, the Dictator, and the Master of Terror*, (New York, 2017), 82
5. Ibid. Victor Sebestyen, 184
6. Disorganization of the October coup: Figes, pp. 484-90; Nikolai Podvoisky, 'Lenin in October', *Krasnaya Gazetta*, 6 November 1927
7. Victor Sebestyen, *Lenin, the Man, the Dictator, and the Master of Terror*, (New York, 2017), 69, 70
8. Richard Pipes, *Communism: A History*, (New York, 2001), 29

9. Victor Sebestyen, *Lenin, the Man, the Dictator, and the Master of Terror*, (New York, 2017), 408. Sebag Montefore, *The Romanov's*

The Truth about Stalin

10. Stephen Kotkin, *Stalin: Volume 1: Paradoxes of Power, 1878–1928*, (Penguin Books, 2014), p. 305
11. Ibid. Stephen Kotkin, p. 290
12. Wikipedia, The Free Encyclopedia, s.v. "Joseph Stalin," (accessed March 12, 2018), https://en.wikipedia.org/wiki/Joseph_Stalin
13. Robert Service, *Stalin: A Biography*. (London: Macmillan, 2004)
14. Montefiore, Simon Sebag, *Stalin: The Court of the Red Tsar*, London: Weidenfeld & Nicolson, 2003
15. Khlevniuk, Oleg V., *Stalin: New Biography of a Dictator*, Translated by Nora Seligman Favorov. New Haven and London: Yale University Press, 2015
16. Richard Pipes, *Communism: A History*, (New York, 2001), 43
17. Ibid. Richard Pipes, 152
18. Famine on the South Siberia, Human Science, RU. 2 (98): 15.
19. Demographic aftermath of the famine in Kazakhstan, Weekly. RU. Jan 1, 2003.
20. Snyder 2010, p. 53. "It seems reasonable to propose a figure of approximately 3.3 million deaths by starvation and hunger-related disease in Soviet Ukraine in 1932–1933".
21. David R. Marples, Heroes and Villains: Creating National History in Contemporary Ukraine. p.50

22. NICCOLÒ PIANCIOLA (2001). "The Collectivization Famine in Kazakhstan, 1931–1933". Harvard Ukrainian Studies. 25 (3–4): 237–251. JSTOR 41036834. PMID 20034146.

23. Volkava, Elena (2012-03-26). "The Kazakh Famine of 1930–33 and the Politics of History in the Post-Soviet Space", Wilson Center. Retrieved 2015-07-09.

24. Stephen Kotkin, *Stalin: Volume 1: Paradoxes of Power, 1878–1928*, (Penguin Books, 2014), p. 290

25. Mikhail Heller and Aleksandr Nekrich, *Utopia in Power: The History of the Soviet Union from 1917 to the Present*, (New York, 1986), 201

Russian Communism

26. Richard Pipes, *Communism: A History*, (New York, 2001), 43

27. Ibid. Richard Pipes, 49

28. Harold Henry Fisher, *The Communist Revolution: An Outline of Strategy and Tactics*, (Stanford University Press, 1955), 13

American Communism

29. Joshua Murovchic, *Heaven on Earth: The Rise and fall of Socialism*, (San Francisco, CA, 2002), 251

30. Ibid. Joshua Murovchic, 250

31. Hoover / Nash, *Freedom Betrayed*, Hoover Institution Press, Stanford University, Stanford California, 2011, 49

32. Keith Sword, *British Reactions to the Soviet Occupation of Eastern Poland in September 1939*, The Slavonic and East European Review, Vol. 69, No. 1 (Jan., 1991), pp. 81-101.

33. Timothy Snyder, *Bloodlands: Europe between Hitler and Stalin*, (London, 2010), 89, 104

34. Leonid Naumov, *Stalin i NKVD*, (Moscow, 2007), 299-300

35. The Journal of Historical Review, Nov.-Dec. 1994 (Vol. 14, No. 6), pages 19-21

36. Hoover / Nash, *Freedom Betrayed*, Hoover Institution Press, Stanford University, Stanford California, 2011, 845

37. Ibid. Hoover / Nash, 845-846, 854

Lend-Lease Act

38. McNeill. *America, Britain and Russia*, 778

39. Motter, T.H. Vail, *The Persian Corridor and Aid to Russia*, Center of Military History (1952), 4–6

40. Deane, John R., *The Strange Alliance: The Story of Our Efforts at Wartime Co-operation with Russia*, (The Viking Press, 1947)

41. Krivosheev, G. F., *Soviet Casualties and Combat Losses in the Twentieth Century*, (London, Greenhill Books, 1997), 252

42. *Russia - British Empire War Assistance*, House of Commons Debates, Hansard, Vol. 421, cc2513-9, 16 April 1946

43. John M. Barr, *World at War 32*, October – November 2013, 27-29

44. Hardesty, Von., *Red Phoenix: The Rise of Soviet Air Power 1941–1945*, Washington, D.C.: Smithsonian Institution, 1991 (first edition 1982), 253

45. Bergstrom, Christer, *Bagration to Berlin: The Final Air Battles in the East: 1944–1945*, Great Britain: Ian Allan, 2008, 132

46. George Racey Jordan, *From Major Jordan's Diaries*, (Belmont, MA Western Islands, 1965), 67, 20

47. Robert Dallek, *Franklin D. Roosevelt and American Foreign Policy, 1932-1945* (New York, Oxford University Press, 1995), 338

48. Weeks, Albert L., *Russia's Life-Saver: Lend-Lease Aid to the U.S.S.R. in World War II,* Lanham, Maryland: Lexington Books, 2004.

49. Khrushchev, Nikita, *Memoirs of Nikita Khrushchev: Commissar, 1918-1945, Volume 1.* Sergei Khrushchev. Pennsylvania State University Press (2005), 675–676.

Pearl Harbor

50. Flynn, John, *The Final Secret of Pearl Harbor* (October 1945)

51. James O. Richardson, *On the Treadmill to Pearl Harbor* (Washington, D.C.: Naval History Division, Department of the Navy, 1973), pp. 307–18, 383–95.

52. 79th Congress, 1st session, Joint Congressional Committee on the Investigation of the Pearl Harbor Attack, (Washington, D.C., U.S. Government Printing Office, 1946), part 1, 425-427

53. James O. Richardson, *On the Treadmill to Pearl Harbor* (Washington, D.C.: Naval History Division, Department of the Navy, 1973), 420

54. Ibid., p. 424

55. William C. Bullitt, "How We Won the War and Lost the Peace," 2 parts. Life (August 30, 1948), pp. 83–97; (September 6, 1948), pp. 86–103.

56. U.S Department of State, *Foreign Relations of the United States: Diplomatic Papers, The Soviet Union, 1933-1939,* (Government Printing Office, Washington D.C., 1952), 224-227

57. 79th Congress, 1st session, *Joint Congressional Committee on the Investigation of the Pearl Harbor Attack*, (U.S. Government Printing Office, Washington, D.C., 1946), part 32, p. 43. Testimony before the Naval Court of Inquiry.

58. Stark testimony before the Roberts Commission, part 12, p. 8.

59. Ingersoll remark at Joint Army-Navy Board November 3 meeting, part 14, 1064

60. Ibid., part 14, pp. 1061–62.

61. Joint Committee, Pearl Harbor Attack, part 36, p. 17, McCollum testimony before the Hewitt Inquiry.

62. Joint Committee, Pearl Harbor Attack, part 2, p. 791, General Miles testimony before the Joint Committee, part 12, p. 262, Tokyo J-19 message to Honolulu #111, translated December 3, 1941.

63. Grew, Joseph C (1944). *Ten Years in Japan*, New York: Simon and Schuster.

64. Percy L. Greaves, Jr., Bettina B. Greaves, ed., *Pearl Harbor: The Seeds and Fruits of Infamy*, Ludwig von Misses Institute, 2010, Auburn, Alabama

65. Wedemeyer Reports, 429-430

66. Department of State Bulletin, December 13, 1941, Washington, DC, Government Printing Office, 1941

67. Ladislas Farago, *Patton: Ordeal and Triumph*, (New York, 1963), 170

68. Ingersoll, Ralph, *Top Secret*, (New York: Harcourt Brace, 1946), 190-191

69. William B. Breuer, *Death of a Nazi Army: The Falaise Pocket*, (Scarborough House, 1985), 295

70. Mark Reardon, *World War II Magazine*, December 2006

71. Manchester, *American Caesar*, 240, 270

72. Ladislas Farago, *Patton: Ordeal and Triumph*, (New York, 1963), 752, 753

73. Ibid. Ladislas Farago, 767, 768

74. Ibid. Ladislas Farago, 770

Soviet Atrocities

75. Joseph Loconte, *FDR at Yalta: Walking with the Devil*, The Weekly Standard, March 2015

76. Antony Beevor, *The Second World War*, (New York, 2012), 204

77. Ibid. Antony Beevor, 336, 360

78. Wikipedia, The Free Encyclopedia, s.v. "Julius Epstein," (accessed February 27, 2019), https://en.wikipedia.org/wiki/Julius_Epstein_(author)

79. Julius Epstein, *Operation Keelhaul: The Story of Forced Repatriation from 1944 to the Present* (Devin-Adair Co., 1973)

80. Jeffrey Rogers Hummel, "Operation Keelhaul - Exposed", *Reason* (1974), 4-9

China and Korea

81. Stephen Kotkin, *Stalin: Volume 1: Paradoxes of Power, 1878–1928*, (Penguin Books, 2014), p. 626

82. Hoover / Nash, *Freedom Betrayed*, Hoover Institution Press, Stanford University, Stanford California, 2011, 483

83. Keith Eiler, An Uncommon Soldier, Hoover Institution, Hoover Digest, October 30, 2001, No. 4

84. Committee on International Relations, "Foreign Assistance Act of 1948," p. 183 (See "U.S. Policy Toward China," December 15, 1945, in Department of State,

Foreign Relations of the United States: Diplomatic Papers, 1945, 9 vols. [Washington: GPO, 1967–69], 7: 770–73

85. Ibid., pp. 184–85

86. Barbara W. Tuchman, *Stilwell and the American Experience in China, 1911-45*, New York, 1971), 646

87. Douglas MacArthur, *Reminiscences*, Naval Institute Press, Annapolis, Maryland, 1964, General Douglas MacArthur Foundation, 321

88. Ibid. Douglas MacArthur, 387

89. Ibid. Douglas MacArthur, 375

90. Ibid. Douglas MacArthur, 368

91. Ibid. Douglas MacArthur, 390

92. Leo Barron, *Patton at the Battle of the Bulge: How the General's Tanks Turned the Tide at Bastogne*

The Balance of Power at the end of World War II

93. Mark O'Neill, *The Soviet Air Force 1917-1991, Soviet Military History* (New York 2002), 163

94. Stephen J. Zaloga, *Soviet / Russian Strategic Nuclear Forces 1945-2000,* Soviet Military History (New York, 2002), 200, 201

95. Christopher C. Lovett, *Soviet Cold War Navy, Soviet Military History* (New York, 2002), 239

96. Mark Harrison, *Accounting for War: Soviet Production, Employment and the Defense Burden, 1940-1945*, 1996

Betrayal and Capitulation

97. M. Stanton Evans, *Blacklisted by History: The Untold Story of Senator Joe McCarthy*, (New York: 2007), 126, FBI Silvermaster file, Vol. 37

98. Hoover / Nash, *Freedom Betrayed*, Hoover
Institution Press, Stanford University, Stanford
California, 2011, 900
99. Ibid. Hoover / Nash, 894
100. Robert K. Wilcox, *Target Patton*, (Washington,
D.C., 2008), 237
101. John Mendelssohn, OSS-NKVD Relationship
1943-1945
102. Douglas Botting and Ian Sayer, *America's Secret
Army: The Untold Story of the Counter Intelligence
Corps*, (London, Fontana Publishers, 1990), 42-47
103. *United States Relations with China*, 766

The Atomic Bomb

104. Perazzo, John, *Barack Obama, The Socialist*,
Frontpage Magazine, September 5, 2012
105. Robert S. Norris, *Racing for the Bomb: General
Leslie S. Groves, The Manhattan Project's Indispensable
Man* (South Royalton, VT: Steerforth Press, 2002), 169
106. Yemelyanov, V. S. *The Making of the Soviet Bomb*,
The Bulletin of Atomic Scientists (Dec. 1987), 40
107. Albrecht, U. *The Development of the First Atomic
Bomb in the USSR. Science, Technology, and the Military*
(Boston, Kluwer Academic Publishers, 1988), 367-70
108. Ibid. Albrecht, 366
109. Leskov, S., *Dividing the Glory of the Fathers*, The
Bulletin of the Atomic Scientists (May 1993), 38
110. Radosh, R., and Breindel, E., *Bombshell: The KGB
Fesses Up*, The New Republic, 10 June 1991, 11
111. Williams, R. C., *Klaus Fuchs, Atom Spy* (Cambridge, Harvard University Press, 1987), 18

112. Hyde, H. M., *The Atom Bomb Spies* (London, Hamish Hamilton, 1980), 91

113. Ibid. Hyde, 56, 91

114. de Toledano, R., *The Greatest Plot in History* (New Rochelle, NY, Arlington House Publishers, 1987), 44

115. George Racey Jordan, *From Major Jordan's Diaries*, (Belmont, MA Western Islands, 1965)

116. Hearings Regarding Shipments of Atomic Materials to Russia During World War Two, House Committee on Un-American Activities, 81st Congress, December 7, 1949, 947

117. Hearings Regarding Shipments of Atomic Materials to Russia During World War Two, House Committee on Un-American Activities, 81st Congress, 1149

118. Additional Sources for Espionage and the Manhattan Project, 1940-1945

Christopher Andrew and Vasili Mitrokhin, *The Sword and the Shield: The Mitrokhin Archive and the Secret History of the KGB* (New York: Basic Books, 1999)

John Earl Haynes and Harvey Klehr, *Venona: Decoding Soviet Espionage in America* (New Haven and London, Yale University Press, 1999)

David Holloway, *Stalin and the Bomb: The Soviet Union and Atomic Energy, 1939-1956* (New Haven, CT, Yale University Press, 1994)

Jeffrey T. Richelson, *A Century of Spies: Intelligence in the Twentieth Century* (New York, Oxford University Press, 1995)

Allen Weinstein and Alexander Vassiliev, *The Haunted Wood: Soviet Espionage in America - the Stalin Era* (New York, Random House, 1999)

Diana West, *American Betrayal: The Secret Assault on Our Nation's Character,* (New York, Saint Martin's Griffin, 2013)

What Could Have Been

119. Larry G. Newman, *General Patton's Premonition*, The American Legion Magazine, July 1962
120. Dikötter, Frank, Mao's Great Famine: The History of China's Most Devastating Catastrophe, 1958–62. Walker & Company, 2010. p. 333
121. Ibid. Dikötter (2010). pp. 298, 304
122. Chang, Jung and Halliday, Jon, *Mao: The Unknown Story*, Jonathan Cape, London, 2005. p. 569
123. Merrill Goldman; Lydia Perry (December 5, 1995). "The Chinese Case: Was It Genocide or Poor Policy?" The Cultural Revolution was modern China's most destructive episode. It is estimated that 100 million people were persecuted and about five to ten million people, mostly intellectuals and party officials lost their lives.
124. Walter E. Williams, Ominous Parallels, August 18, 2011
125. David Boaz, *Hitler, Mussolini, Roosevelt*, Reason Magazine, October 2007
126. Douglas MacArthur, *Reminiscences*, Naval Institute Press, Annapolis, Maryland, 1964, General Douglas MacArthur Foundation, 414-415

Index

A

Admiral Kimmel 51
Admiral Richardson - relieved of command 50
Admiral Sir Tom Phillips 47
Admiral Wilkinson 54
Ambassador Bullitt 51
American Communism 34
American press 78
American soldier 61
Animal Farm 29
Appell, Donald 105
AP US History 97
Argentan 62
Atomic bomb 90, 98

B

Battle of the Bulge 63
BBC poll 10
Bell P-39 Airacobra 46
Beria, Lavrentiy 103, 105
Bessarabia 41
Betrayal and Capitulation 93
Bolshevik Party 29
Bolshevik revolution 20
Bolshevism 18
Bourgeois 7

D

Das Capital 11
Davies, Joseph 95
Deng Xiaoping 32
Dialectical materialism 6
Diffusion 101
Dodd, Thomas 80
Dr. Fred Schwarz 14
Duranty, Walter 95

E

Eisenhower, Dwight D. 63, 69
Encyclopedia of Military History 83
Engels, Friedrich 10
Epstein, Julius 69
Evil - defined 5

F

Failures of communism 30
Falaise Gap 61
Famine 31
FBI 96, 109
FBI Director Hoover 93
Fourier, Charles 35
Four Modernizations 32
Fuchs, Klaus 102

G

Gavin, James 63
General Antonov 65
General Eisenhower - Operation Keelhaul 72
General George S. Patton 84
General Leslie Groves 99
General Leslie Groves - and Lend-Lease 105
General Lin Piao 81
General MacArthur 65, 86
    and China policy failure 79
    and Korean War 81
    on nationalism 118
General Mark Clark 65

The Truth about Lenin 17
The Truth about Stalin 24
Third Army 62, 66, 85
Totalitarianism - defined 9
Trotsky 23, 30
        and assassination 27
Truman 87
Truman administration 76
Truman, Harry S. 108
Tsar Nicholas II and his family execution 23
Tu-4 bomber 89

U

Ukraine - famine 31
Unchangeable law of history 6
Uranium 101
U.S. Military Academy at West Point 86

V

Vietnam War 114

W

What is to be Done? 18
Wilcox, Robert K. 97
Works Progress Administration (WPA) 95
World War I 114

Y

Yalta - Far Eastern Agreement 76
Yalu River 81
You can Trust the Communists to be Communists 14

Z

Zhukov 68

www.ingramcontent.com/pod-product-compliance
Lightning Source LLC
Chambersburg PA
CBHW021128020426
42331CB00005B/662